I CAN GET PAID FOR *THAT?*

Smith Street Books

99 creative careers
to live a life less ordinary

Jo Stewart

Contents

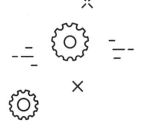

Introduction

Hi there! This compendium of out-of-the-ordinary career options was compiled to help you open up to all of the incredible possibilities out there. Some of the featured careers may not be for you (taxidermy anyone?), others may be the perfect fit for your skill set, interests, talents and curiosities. Regardless of what you think of each of the careers featured in this book, as a whole they represent opportunity in many brilliant forms.

In my travels I've met, worked with and heard about a number of people working in outrageous fields. From science to hospitality, the arts and government, there are many people who have carved out extraordinary roles for themselves. Some have invested in decades of education to get where they are, while others have made up their own job titles and thrived without spending a minute on studying.

When you're trying to choose a suitable career it can sometimes feel like the pathways are set, the roadblocks are in place and the dice are loaded against you. This book aims to blow the cobwebs out of the neural pathways that have led you to believe you can't dedicate your life to working the way you want.

When we think about future career possibilities, many of us get stuck on the reasons why a certain career *won't* work out for us. Of course, that hard old chestnut of practicality has its place in our lives (begrudgingly so), but immediately writing off a career as for someone else – someone smarter, or luckier, or more privileged – is both self-defeating and a little bit tragic when you consider how much of our lives we spend at work.

Obviously, life is a fickle thing and many career successes can be attributed to an unpredictable cluster of uncontrollable factors. Luck, timing, personal background, privilege and location can all play a part in where your career takes you. But other factors that you can control – such as working hard, being committed to a path and investing in education – can also have an impact on your career path and your ability to earn money.

Not all of us can get what we want in life, this is true. However, this book encourages you to take a moment to see all the possibilities in the world. Because there's more than enough people ready to tell you what you can't do, who you can't be, and what's not suitable for you. This book is a big middle finger to all the negative Nellies, naysayers and dream-crushers who never took a chance or were never given the opportunity to follow the career they wanted, so think it's cool to discourage others. This book will give you a sweet taste of all the bizarre, strange, cool, funny, weird, outlandish, interesting, unbelievable things that people get paid to do.

I sincerely hope that, like me, you end up getting paid to do awesome things sometime soon (but if you want to be an accountant that's cool too).

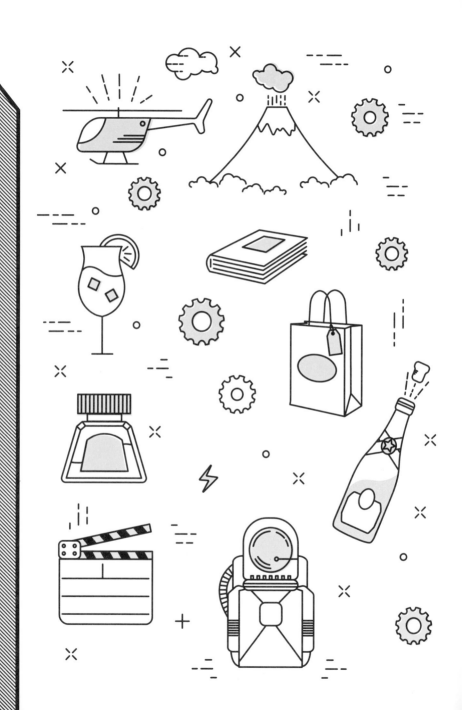

Airplane repossession agent

Thinking of a creative way to put a pilot's licence to good use? Many people enter the military and fly fighter jets, some join commercial airlines and ferry tourists around the world, and then there are the pilots that get into the totally wild repossession game. Yes, airline repossession is a thing and it's quite a big business.

In what has to be one of the most bizarre careers to ever exist on the planet, airplane repossession agents are trained, registered pilots who work with repossession companies to recover aircraft from people who haven't paid their bills. Just like your car can be repossessed if you neglect to make the payments, airplanes can also be repossessed. (Newsflash: you can't just sign up for a multi-million dollar aircraft and then run out on the bill when you hit financial trouble.)

People experience financial difficulties for a number of reasons – wildly fluctuating incomes, bad investments, financial mismanagement, stock market crashes, costly court cases – and this is why airplane repossession is a big game. Anyone who has watched the Discovery Channel's *Airplane Repo* will know that banks are ruthless when it comes to recovering debts from people who have defaulted on their loans, and the wealthy are no exception.

So how does airplane repossession work? Well, once the necessary paperwork has been filled out and the aircraft located, a pilot and repo team are flown in to repossess the plane and return the asset to the bank, which will go on to sell the aircraft to recoup loan costs. Depending on the jurisdiction, local authorities (police and airports) are notified and then the repo can occur once all the safety checks are completed. Possessing a licence to fly the aircraft, the pilot repossesses the plane by towing or flying it to another location. It's a huge logistical operation only suited to calm, precise and analytical pilots with an understanding of processes and a respect for following protocol. Luckily pilots tend to have already cultivated these skills in flying school.

No two cases are the same in this type of role. One day you could repossess a multi-million dollar Learjet, the next a single-engine Cessna. Flying the plane to another location is only a part of the role, with much time spent doing detective work, such as locating the plane and its log books, communicating with owners, assessing the safety of flying the aircraft and liaising with regulatory bodies. Sure, it's a high-stakes business, but this job doesn't really involve penetrating barbed wire fences at airports and stealing keys from the back pockets of unsuspecting owners.

Repossession agents are commonly paid a fee per repossessed aircraft so, depending on how hard you work, it can be quite lucrative. Since all piloting work is well paid, the repossession work is in line with what pilots can command for other commercial flying work. Despite this, it's easy to see the allure of this role. You can tell people you're a pilot for American Airlines or British Airways, or you can say you're an airline repossession agent. While both kinds of pilots are no doubt full of stories of mile-high adventures, airline repossession agents have the cool factor commercial pilots never will.

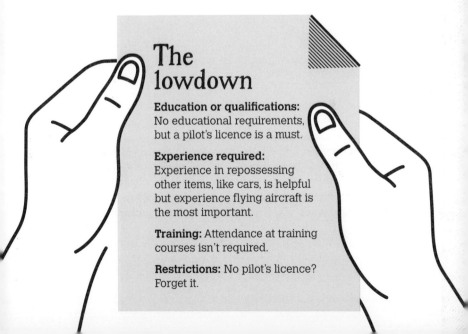

The lowdown

Education or qualifications:
No educational requirements, but a pilot's licence is a must.

Experience required:
Experience in repossessing other items, like cars, is helpful but experience flying aircraft is the most important.

Training: Attendance at training courses isn't required.

Restrictions: No pilot's licence? Forget it.

Animator

Fancy working on a Disney movie? Or what about a Pixar film? Or perhaps the next big video game to sweep the world? Animators are behind some of the world's most endearing movies and addictive video games and, with the explosion in digital technology – along with the public's enduring love for animated features – good animators are in hot demand.

Working to create visual effects for films, video games, television shows and commercials, animators use a range of software programs, with the exception of a few old-school animators still using raw materials, to bring things to life on the screen for the public's enjoyment and entertainment.

When thinking about the impact that animated movies have had on your childhood (and adulthood) it's easy to see how important the role of an animator truly is. There's *Toy Story, Finding Nemo, Spirited Away, Shrek, Fantastic Mr. Fox, The Little Mermaid* and *The Lion King*. Children's movies aside, animation is also often used in movies for adults, with *Avatar* being a good example of the role it plays. And what about television? Imagine life without *South Park, The Simpsons, Family Guy* and *The Ren & Stimpy Show*?

Surely you're now convinced of the monumental impact that animators have had on pop culture and are desperate to sign on to a life as an animator. Well, hold your horses because despite appearances it's not a career full of fun and games. Animators need to spend years studying the craft before being able to gain work with studios or set up their own production companies. It's a painstaking process to learn all the techniques and computer programs used in the industry. Then there's understanding the basics of film and television production. On top of that, as a highly competitive industry, there are plenty of animators out there studying and learning the craft too.

If you make it in the industry there are many paths to take. Many animators work for themselves on a freelance basis. Financial security is notoriously tough for freelancers, but working in your own business allows you the freedom and flexibility to work wherever you want, whether that is at home or within a studio. Freelance work also allows a greater level of agency than working with a production company for a salary. Freelancers get to work on a wider variety of productions, while salaried animators working as employees typically work on a narrower range of projects.

On the flipside, salaried roles offer more job security and if Pixar came knocking on your door with the role of a lifetime, you'd have to be nuts to pass it up. With top animators able to command six-figure salaries, animation can pay financial dividends if you show creativity, diligence, reliability and high levels of skill. Of course, a career isn't all about the money – you need a reason to get up in the morning too. Thankfully animation offers the chance to be highly creative, to entertain people and perhaps even contribute to a production that people that still watch decades later. You could also be responsible for the next *Frozen* and then have to explain yourself to a whole generation of annoyed parents, but them's the breaks of working in the fickle old world of entertainment.

The lowdown

Education or qualifications: No degree necessary but qualifications from a film school or multimedia arts college would be helpful.

Experience required: Experience animating your own shorts is helpful when applying for animation jobs. Putting together a show reel of your amateur work will show you have the experience to work on bigger projects.

Training: Animation classes and workshops are taught all over the world and via online courses.

Restrictions: None.

Antarctic postal officer

Working in a post office may just be your idea of hell, but what about working in a post office surrounded by glaciers, the roaring ocean and hundreds of penguins? Now you're talking!

Located on remote, windswept Goudier Island, Antarctica, the southernmost post office in the world operates from November to March and is staffed by a fresh batch of recruits each year. Run by the United Kingdom Antarctic Heritage Trust, Port Lockroy Post Office is much, much more than your average post office. Yes, you can buy postcards and stamps, but with the space encompassing the historic scientific research station known as 'Base A', working at Port Lockroy involves a little bit of everything: office administration, museum maintenance, tour guiding and retail assistance.

If a large cruise ship arrives, then you'll need to show passengers around the museum, sell postcards and merchandise, press cute penguin stamps into passports and answer a lot of questions about your job. On a quieter day, you might be expected to clean the museum, fill out paperwork or take part in maintenance work on your living quarters. Some post office workers also assist researchers by keeping an eye on local penguin numbers.

The remote nature of the post office means workers must live on-site, in simple, well-constructed huts located behind the post office. As a small island with next-to-no facilities, you must be comfortable with living and working with strangers in isolation for six months of the year. This may sound like a dream job for introverts, but extroverted peeps might find themselves challenged by the lack of social interaction or entertainment. There are no cafes, bars or pubs to hang out in, no gigs to rock out to, no shopping centres to browse at and no neighbours to chat to. This may seem confronting, but you will be able to take in views of some of the wildest seas in the world, get up close and personal with penguins on a daily basis, and meet lots of interesting people who'll stop by to send a postcard from the bottom of the world.

There is plenty of competition for these roles. Although you don't need to be a UK citizen to apply, it helps to be located there (or nearby) as the interviews and training take place in Cambridge. The application process covers a wide range of criteria to ensure the right people end up with the job. Of course, having the mental capacity to work in a remote environment is a must.

While not a long-term profession by any means, living and working in Antarctica is a real coup and a life experience that will provide enough stories to see you through many dates, dinner parties and meet-the-parents situations. Trust me, saying you've worked in a post office in Antarctica is a real ice breaker.

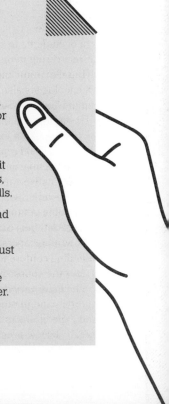

The lowdown

Education or qualifications: No formal education requirements are required but a good command of English is a necessity for this role.

Experience required: Applicants don't require any postal service experience but it helps to have a wide variety of capabilities, from customer service to maintenance skills.

Training: Successful applicants must attend a six-day training session in the UK.

Restrictions: None, although applicants must be available to fulfil a six-month contract in Antarctica, living and working in a place without mains power, heat or running water.

Archaeologist

If you've ever been accused of living in the past, then perhaps you should put your fascination with the past to good use and become an archaeologist.

From unearthing the skeletons of people who walked the Earth thousands of years ago, to uncovering the remains of houses that once stood centuries before, archaeologists study how people lived in the past by finding and examining the remains of previous civilisations.

The field of archaeology is one of the more popular, accessible forms of science out there. Captivating everyone from high school students to seniors, archaeologists have been responsible for recovering items from the *Titanic*, discovering the tomb of Tutankhamun and uncovering the devastation of Pompeii. Archaeologists also found the Dead Sea Scrolls, the Rosetta Stone, and the Tomb of Sunken Skulls.

Unsurprisingly, the life of an archaeologist is absolutely nothing like the life of Indiana Jones. The reality of archaeology is very different from Hollywood representations. Pulling yourself out of a pit of snakes, outsmarting bad guys with guns, and being chased by arrow-wielding natives just doesn't figure in the life of an archaeologist. Using a leather whip and wearing a fedora hat also isn't necessary. Sure, some get to work on archaeological digs in exotic places throughout their careers, but many hours are spent sitting at a desk writing papers, reading journals and sifting through research. Attending conferences is another less thrilling part of the job.

Over the course of decades, the career of an archaeologist can be quite varied. Many archaeologists work at universities as lecturers and in other academic roles, others write books, some lead expeditions to complete field work in remote places, and the rare, lucky few progress into television work hosting shows on archaeology and history. Archaeologists often advise governments and engineers on building projects, and work with cultural institutions like museums and galleries to put together exhibitions and programs.

As a career, this branch of science requires years and years of study. Apart from academic study, archaeologists must also develop the technical skills needed to participate on excavation sites and to work in laboratories. From using geographic information systems to record finds, to conducting laboratory tests such as radiocarbon dating, as well as having the skills to clean and preserve the artefacts, this is a career that requires a very broad skill set.

At the end of their career, an archaeologist ends up a very well-rounded individual. Part educator, part writer, part curator, part excavator, this is a science role perfect for passionate time travellers with a fascination for all things old and musty. No, you don't get to crack a whip like Indiana Jones but you might end up uncovering a relic that changes our understanding of a place or people. Pretty cool, right?

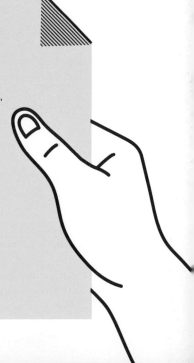

The lowdown

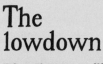

Education or qualifications:
Degree in archaeology is required, with postgraduate qualifications highly regarded.

Experience required: Experience working in the field on archaeological sites and digs is necessary.

Training: Archaeologists receive training on field-work techniques while completing their degrees and interning at places such as museums.

Restrictions: None.

Art conservator

In 2012 an elderly amateur restorer rose to internet fame after completing a hilarious hatchet job on a fresco that adorned the walls of a church in Spain. If the world learned anything from this accidental destruction of a 19th century fresco at the hands of a pensioner with a whole load of good intentions but zero restoration skills, it's that art conservation and restoration should never be left in the hands of amateurs.

A great career choice for anyone with a genuine love of art who doesn't necessarily want to become an artist, thousands of art conservators are currently working all over the world. Working on repairing canvas tears, surface cleaning, reframing, retouching, and making sure artworks are secure before being removed from a house or gallery, an art conservator ensures that works of art are kept in good condition.

The painstaking process of art conservation and restoration is best left in the hands of experienced, talented conservators who have invested years of their life studying and working in this field. Apart from having the technical skills and know-how to restore artworks, conservators and restorers need to have a steady hand and a patient mind, as this type of meticulous work can't be rushed. An understanding of ethics is also required, as is some basic scientific knowledge, as many chemical processes are used in conservation work.

Some art conservators run their own businesses restoring work for private clients or consulting to galleries, auction houses and public institutions. Others work on a full-time basis in-house for large art galleries and museums that require conservation work all year round. Such is the detailed, specialised nature of the job, most conservators work in one medium only with painting, textiles, paper, ceramics and objects being the main categories. Some also choose to specialise in preventative conservation – the process of identifying potential risks and preventing damage to art before it happens.

Working in large, influential galleries, like the Guggenheim, the Louvre, or the Tate Modern, offers the best chance to handle some of the most influential, and expensive, works of art in the world. Imagine advising on how to successfully move and hang a priceless Picasso. Or repair damage to a watercolour by Monet. Or give one of Turner's oil paintings a bit of a clean.

This career gives you the chance to interact with and contribute to the art world in ways most people would never dream of. Whether restoring a faded painting to its former glory, repairing fractures in a priceless Ming Dynasty vase, or helping a wealthy philanthropist ensure their private gallery is moved and then displayed in the safest and most effective way, this career is an unfathomably rewarding one for art lovers.

The lowdown

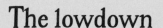

Education or qualifications: Most art conservators have a Master of Arts or equivalent degree. Postgraduate courses in art conservation are taught in most major cities around the world.

Experience required: Extensive experience studying, assessing, preserving and restoring artworks in either private or public galleries. Many art conservators start out as volunteers within art conservation departments of museums and galleries.

Training: Many art and education institutions offer training in art conservation. An undergraduate degree in arts or fine arts is usually required before embarking on further study.

Restrictions: None.

Art therapist

Think that art is nothing more than a beautiful yet frivolous luxury? Well, you'd be dead wrong because art has the power to change lives, heal wounds and help people in ways medication often can't. If you have a flair for art and a genuine desire to help others heal, then art therapy might be a career worth sketching into your life plan.

Helping both adults and children to work through psychological issues using art techniques, art therapy is a psychotherapeutic form of therapy commonly used all over the world. Art therapists work with clients individually and also in groups, especially family groups. Using techniques like journaling, painting, building sculptures and creating collages, art therapy gives people an outlet to work through troubling emotions and move towards a healthier mind space.

The perfect form of therapy for reluctant talkers, art therapy is known to improve communication skills, reduce anxiety, boost confidence levels and improve self-esteem. Used to manage conditions, disorders and issues such as post-traumatic stress disorder (PTSD), alcohol and drug dependence, depression, anxiety and grief, art therapy isn't just a fluffy exercise – it's a legitimate form of therapy that produces results.

As such, becoming an art therapist is a serious undertaking. You need much more than an interest in art and some empathy to be able to operate as a licensed, certified art therapist. Many art therapists have a Masters in art therapy; others choose to study traditional psychology or psychiatry and then transition into art therapy. With the lives of vulnerable people in your hands, it's an important role only suited to people with the right combination of technical, clinical and personal skills.

Having an understanding of psychology is a given, but you'll also need to be patient, non-judgemental, open-minded and caring. Possessing a sound knowledge of professional ethics is important, as is knowing the ins and outs of art therapy practices and how to deal with confronting situations.

With art therapists positively impacting everyone from the bereaved to those living with a serious mental illness, this creative career is a highly rewarding one. Having the ability to assist clients on the road to better mental health must surely be an awesome way to contribute to society through the arts. Whether practising in hospitals or privately in an office, studio or clinic, art therapists have an affect on the lives of their clients on a daily basis. Could there be a better way to put a love of art to good use? Probably not.

The lowdown

Education or qualifications: Depending on what country you're practising in, a Master's degree in Art Therapy is usually required to become a licensed, certified art therapist.

Experience required: Previous experience as a counsellor or psychologist would help. Otherwise, degrees in art therapy usually include practical experience modules that include placements at hospitals, clinics and community centres.

Training: Most art therapy degrees include training modules and internships within medical practices.

Restrictions: Criminal record checks apply for this profession.

Ballet dancer

Are you tough as nails? Do you have what it takes to sign up to one of the most physically and mentally demanding careers on the planet? No, I'm not talking about joining the Special Forces (or becoming an elementary school teacher). I'm talking about ballet dancing.

Despite all the grace, elegance and tutu-wearing this profession entails, anyone who has watched *Black Swan* will realise that this is one of the most brutally competitive careers anyone could follow. It is for this reason that you'll rarely see a 'Wanted: Ballet Dancer' job advertised in the local rag. Ballet dancers get their roles by enduring an intense audition process designed to mine the very best talent out of the already freakishly talented pool of candidates.

Usually starting out very young (even toddlers can attend classes), ballet dancers sign over their whole lives to the pursuit of perfection. Following a super strict diet and exercise regime, ballet dancers push themselves to physical and emotional limits unheard of in most other professions. The intent of most dancers is to nab the lead role, which means hours and hours of training and rehearsing to learn the steps and manoeuvres required to nail the part.

Failure, rejection, pain and deprivation are a huge part of being a ballet dancer, so mammoth amounts of stamina, endurance and single-mindedness are needed to follow this punishing career path. If you've made it this far and aren't put off, then it's important to know that there are also plenty of payoffs from pursuing a life as a ballet dancer.

Successful ballet dancers have good earning power, get to travel to the world, and work with respected dancers, choreographers and directors. They get to use their bodies in ways most of the population never will and contribute to an artistic pursuit beloved by many.

If you rise to the very top of this profession, you'll get to experience the rare pleasure of performing around the world in iconic spaces, such as London's Royal Opera House, New York's Metropolitan Opera House and Shanghai's Grand Theatre. A rigid rehearsal structure must be followed, but there's still plenty of room for creativity. You could be a sugar plum fairy in *The Nutcracker*, a woman of many contradictions in *Giselle*, or a star-crossed lover in *Romeo and Juliet*. Working with directors, ballet dancers can interpret their characters in a number of ways, infusing their performance with their own special brand of magic to make audiences laugh, cry and ponder the wonders of the world.

Dancing at an elite level takes its toll on the body, so most only stay at the top for a few years. Even though this profession offers little career longevity, dancers are usually involved with ballet for life. Many ballet dancers end up transitioning into teaching roles, either setting up their own ballet studios or working with production companies as choreographers or instructors. In many ways, joining the ballet world is a bit like joining a gang. Once you're a ballet dancer, you're always a ballet dancer at heart. If that sounds like you, don those leg warmers and start stretching.

The lowdown

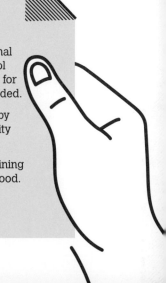

Education or qualifications: Most professional ballet dancers progress through ballet school until they reach the top and start performing for paying audiences. Academic ability isn't needed.

Experience required: Experience is gained by performing with ballet schools and community theatres, then larger ballet companies.

Training: Many years of serious physical training is essential, normally starting in early childhood.

Restrictions: None, apart from the obvious physical restrictions.

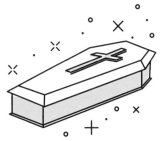

Body farm researcher

Warning: You'd be hard pressed to find a more macabre job on the planet than this one. However, if you've got a fascination for forensics, an enquiring mind and don't gag easily, then this could be the perfect career to allow you to exercise your curiosity while assisting in the process of solving crimes.

So what exactly is a body farm? Well, whenever you see a news report about a murder or suspicious death, investigators often estimate when, and sometimes how, they think the death occurred. Body farm research facilities play a big part in accurately estimating the time and cause of death. As bodies decompose it gets harder and harder to determine these factors, making solving the crime and finding the perpetrator a more challenging prospect. Body farms take cadavers that have been donated to science, arrange them in different burial scenarios – above ground, below ground and sometimes in water – and then take notes on the various stages of decomposition that occur over time. Nobody would ever accuse this job of being a glamorous one!

Body farms are usually located in rural areas that are kept out of the public eye. Security is tight and the exact location is not advertised to the public to avoid interference with the bodies or curious visitors. Body farms aren't without their detractors either, so housing a research facility like this somewhere remote, away from the public eye, is a good idea to ensure that others are not impacted by it.

So what types of people work at body farms? Well, just because you're a little fascinated by death doesn't mean you are the right fit for a job at a body farm. As a scientific research facility, you will need to have studied one of the forensic sciences to be able to work on a body farm. You'll need to have extensive experience working in labs, under the guidance of trained forensic anthropologists.

If you fit the bill, your work will contribute to society in many important ways. From helping to train cadaver-detecting canines to assisting law enforcement in being able to pinpoint a time of death, information gathered from body farm research is incredibly valuable. Some people may be affronted or shocked by your career choice, but hey, we're all going to die, right?

With only a handful of body farms in the world – mostly located in the USA and Australia – this is a niche profession for scientists with a niche set of skills (and very, very strong stomachs). Nevertheless, if you think you've got what it takes to work in a place full of rotting corpses, then, a) you're a better person than me and, b) you better start acing your science tests because you're going to need the best grades to follow forensic anthropology all the way to the body farm.

The lowdown

Education or qualifications: Tertiary qualifications in forensics are necessary.

Experience required: Experience working in laboratories, especially in the area of forensics.

Training: On-the-job training is provided in labs while studying. A strong understanding of the ethics of working with cadavers is essential and mostly gained while studying and training in forensics.

Restrictions: Depending on where you are working, criminal record checks may be required to work in this area.

Body paint artist

Now here's a boundary-breaking career that will really raise the eyebrows of your parents. If you're artistically inclined and totally down with working with naked people, then the liberated life of a body paint artist is a career path well worth following.

Painting bodies and faces for live performances, commercials, magazine covers and film and television series, body paint artists use considerable skill and a whole load of creativity to transform skin into living, breathing, moving works of art.

From turning a woman into an elaborately painted Hindu goddess, to transforming a man into a brain-eating zombie covered in rotting flesh, body paint artists tend to run their own businesses, offering their highly specialised services to the entertainment, advertising and modelling industries.

Pathways to this career are varied, as there's no set amount of study required to become a body paint artist. Some successful body paint artists have degrees in fine arts, others made the transition from make-up artist to body paint artist. Essentially, it's the type of career move propelled by passion and experimentation, not tertiary study.

Sure, the idea of painting naked bodies might sound like a whole load of fun, but it's important to remember that this career is also a whole load of hard work and definitely not suited to everyone. Patience is required to perfect this art form and when considering body paint artists have access to people in vulnerable positions, they also need to be professional and discreet at all times. If you're a prude or prone to giggling at the sight of a naked body, then this is absolutely not the career for you.

As business owners, body paint artists need to be able to market themselves, build networks and make connections in a variety of industries in order to gain enough work to sustain themselves. With the body paint art process taking many hours to complete, having a good handle on pricing will also help – this isn't a cheap art form and should be priced accordingly.

One of the best parts of this job is dreaming up new characters and new ways to tell stories through body paint. Just like artists who work with watercolours on canvas, or spray paint on walls, body paint artists work to create new worlds for their audience to delight in, recoil from or admire. The only difference is they are painting flesh.

Even though the market for body paint art is quite small, there aren't many body paint artists out there, so if you've got creative talent, artistic ability and good business instincts, there's a strong chance you'll be able to land some clients and build a tidy little career from painting the bodies of strangers. On the flipside, it would be tricky to make a start in this career as a relative unknown, so you should be aware of the difficulties of starting an artistic enterprise.

If and when you make it, you'll get to work in one of the coolest emerging industries on the planet, potentially painting the bodies of famous people, travelling the world to paint people at festivals, working on Hollywood film sets, having your work on the cover of *Rolling Stone*. Essentially, this is a career with lots of potential.

The lowdown

Education or qualifications: None.

Experience required: Experience in the arts sector is favourable, as is experience painting and applying stage make-up.

Training: Body paint workshops and classes can be found in some cities. Make-up application courses will also help with this career.

Restrictions: None.

Brewer

Crack into a cold one, get stuck into a bottle of chugger's delight, get hit by the liquid wrecking ball. Call it what you like, beer is one of the world's most beloved drinks and being a brewer is one of those mythical jobs that many people dream of doing but strangely enough don't follow up on. I'm here to tell you that being paid to create and bottle liquid sunshine is entirely possible and a career well worth pursuing.

You'd have to be living under a rock to not notice the recent explosion in craft brewing over the past few years. Once upon a time, beer drinkers had limited choices as mainstream brands dominated the offering, but now beer lovers are living in the golden age of craft brewing, where taprooms overflow with golden ale, bars stock hundreds of varieties of bottled brews from all over the world and weak, watery, bland beers are relegated to being stocked at gas stations (and your clueless uncle's fridge).

These days, craft beer flavours are being taken in previously unheard of directions. Much to the disgust of the older generation, creative craft brewers are turning out funky flavours of beer that push boundaries and sometimes even defy logic. Gone are the days where a crisp lager or a dark stout were the only options worth considering. Nowadays, we live in a glorious wonderland where weird and whacky beer flavours deliver more much than a bottle of Budweiser ever will.

Craft brewers are an experimental bunch unafraid to get creative with their concoctions, from beer that tastes like a taco, to zingy beers that have a chilli aftertaste, refreshing ales with notes of passionfruit and even beer that tastes exactly like a jam donut (how do they do it?). There's even a beer on the market that tastes like ambergris. (For the people among us who didn't study marine biology, ambergris is whale vomit – that one is best left on the shelf, trust me.) Women are getting into the brewing action too.

So how do you become a brewer? Well, the good news is that the recent resurgence of craft brewing means that this is a growing industry with more opportunities than ever before. There's a real need for trained brewers to enter the industry. Getting a feel for it by experimenting with home brewing is a great start. Brewing courses are also available in many cities around the world, and cover everything from brewing basics to more complicated techniques for producing specialist beers.

While you may be tempted to think that the life of a brewer is like living in a magical utopia, it's time to take off your beer goggles and see it for what it really is. The reality is that brewing is actually really hard work. The hours are often long, with early starts to boot. The work is physically taxing and the production schedules relentless (a lot of people need a drink!). There is little margin for error in this job.

But, if you're unafraid of hard work, know your hops from your malted barley, and have a passion for creating liquids that make people happy (and make some people do stupid things) then go forth and brew yourself up a career worth bragging about.

The lowdown

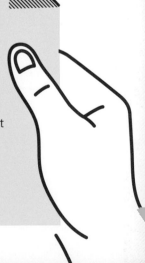

Education or qualifications: No formal degrees are required.

Experience required: Experience working in a commercial brewery is needed. Home brewing experience and knowledge is also helpful.

Training: Brewing courses can be found in most countries in the world. Some breweries offer apprenticeships or entry-level roles where on-the-job training is included.

Restrictions: Must be able to drink alcohol.

Calligrapher

If anyone has ever commented on your perfect penmanship, then don't put your talent for handwriting to waste – turn it into a profession by becoming a professional calligrapher.

While it would be tempting to think that beautiful, cursive handwriting is a thing of the past (we are living in the digital age after all), calligraphy is most certainly not dead. Sure, the profession has changed somewhat since the arrival of digital printers and computers, but there's still a need for calligraphers in this world.

From hand writing beautiful wedding invitations and penning place card settings and commemorative menus for black tie functions, to designing logos and corporate branding in handwritten fonts, there is a variety of work on offer for talented calligraphers. Usually running their own businesses or working on a freelance basis, calligraphers often work on a variety of projects over the course of a year, using a wide range of font styles perfected over years of practice.

Perfecting fonts is the name of the game for a calligrapher and, whether they're coming up with new, inventive font styles or recreating the classics, hours and hours of practice is essential to nailing this career. With so many variables – ink quality, paper stock, paper width – to contend with, the only thing that will get you through this delicate profession is having the depth of experience to handle different calligraphy projects. Having patience helps, as does possessing a steady hand and the ability to stick to the brief, as there's no point giving a client an Art Deco-style font if they wanted something more modern.

So apart from sitting around writing beautifully all day, what else do calligraphers do to make money? As a niche profession, calligraphers must innovate in order to make a healthy income from their work. Aside from their core work, some teach calligraphy workshops, while others make handcrafted greeting cards to sell at stationery stores and online via website such as Etsy. Offering a wide range of bespoke services means calligraphers have many avenues to make their career profitable (because sitting in your studio waiting for masses of people to roll in asking for hand lettering just isn't going to happen).

The life of a calligrapher is lived in the pursuit of creating beautiful things. In a time where mass production and globalisation appear to rule the world, thankfully there are still calligraphers out there.

The lowdown

Education or qualifications: None.

Experience required: None.

Training: Calligraphy classes and workshops can be found in most major cities. There are also plenty of instructive books on the art form.

Restrictions: None.

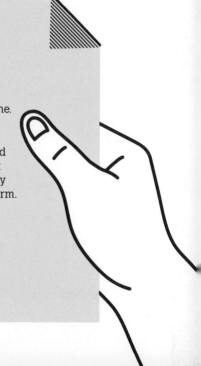

Celebrity agent

If you fancy yourself as a bit of a well-connected rainmaker who loves the art of negotiation and has a killer instinct for securing red hot deals, then turning your talents into a business representing celebrities could be a lucrative, creative career path.

Being a celebrity agent, or talent manager, involves working with a wide range of celebrities, artists and other performers in order to secure work for them at the best rates. Relying on instinct, industry knowledge and a full list of contacts, agents use their powers of persuasion and negotiation to arrange auditions, secure contracts and pull off deals for their clients.

Whether they're representing the latest baseball prodigy, a Hollywood star, a fashion model or a best-selling novelist, agents need to possess confidence, persistence and an eye for opportunity. Building strong relationships with the key players in the industry, such as film producers and directors, casting agents, sports team owners and publishers, is essential to getting the inside run on new opportunities, as is delivering results for your clients who want to be cast in the best roles, join the best sports teams and earn truckloads of money for endorsements.

Despite confidence and connections playing an important part, not all agents are like Ari Gold from *Entourage*. Sure, there are some classic old-school agents still operating in Hollywood but, as a profession, agents are a bit of a mixed bag. So getting about in a Ferrari and wearing designer suits isn't a necessity, but working hard to secure the best deals for your clients is. With most agents taking a fair cut of their clients' earnings, it's in their best interests to ink good deals and stay hungry for new opportunities anyway.

So how do you become an agent? There's no hard and fast way to become a celebrity agent. Some agents study degrees in arts, management or business, although this is not necessary. Some start out in entry-level positions with talent agencies and work their way up to agent level once they have enough experience, industry contacts and know-how to take on their own client list.

With celebrity agents either working with big talent agencies or in their businesses, top-performing agents can end up earning in the millions, especially if they are representing actors or sportspeople that command big pay days. Other benefits include being invited to exclusive industry functions and parties, frequent travel and getting to work with celebrities (although that could be a negative depending on which celebrity we're talking about). Apart from all the money, travel and parties on offer, agents also get to influence the outcomes of cultural history. It's not a stretch to say that agents have had a hand in influencing everything from placing athletes in sporting teams that have gone on to win premierships to ensuring Oscar-winning actors ended up playing the part that landed them the gold statue. So yeah, celebrity agents don't just secure big deals, they kind of *are* big deals themselves.

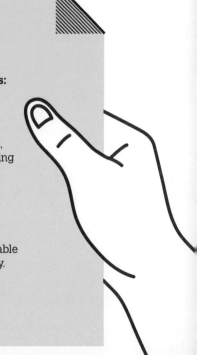

The lowdown

Education or qualifications: None.

Experience required: Experience managing the careers of others is needed, as well as experience working in the field of the people you're representing, for example, sports, publishing, entertainment.

Training: None. There are management courses available but training isn't a necessity.

Restrictions: None.

Celebrity stylist

If you're the type of person who devours every new issue of *Vogue* and loves putting together killer looks for friends, then the enviable career of a celebrity stylist is worth pursuing.

Much more than just playing with clothes for a living, the life of a celebrity stylist is multifaceted. From putting together looks for red carpet events such as movie premieres and awards presentations, to working on photoshoots for magazine editorial and advertising campaigns, stylists must have a specific skill set that goes beyond a passion for fashion.

Apart from staying on top of the latest trends in fashion, celebrity stylists need to know what clothing styles suit different body types and how to tailor looks that project certain qualities. If a celebrity is going through a scandal, then watch the conservative, buttoned-up shirt and clean-shaven face come out for the courtroom appearances. If a child star wants to wash that Disney role right out of their hair, then in come the leather, piercings, tattoos and wrecking ball. Make no mistake – celebrity stylists are an important cog in the wheel of the publicity machine.

When not working with clients, celebrity stylists spend their time building relationships with labels and designers, attending fashion shows, blogging and managing their social media accounts. Most stylists run their own empires, so there's flexibility and the chance to earn really good money on offer, but with that comes a lot of hard work and uncertainty when you're starting out and haven't yet built a profile.

If you're keen to break into celebrity styling, then you'll need to cultivate diplomacy (try telling that A-list star that the dress they love does them no favours), a good work ethic (styling isn't a nine-to-five job so you'll be expected to be on-call for late-night awards ceremony outfit 'emergencies'), and a can-do attitude (to nab those rare Harry Winston jewels for a client before some other star does). You'll also need to have supreme confidence in your talents in order to build a network and land A-list clients. Of course, you'll actually need to know how to put together everything from seasonal wardrobes to glamorous red carpet one-offs. An understanding of the editorial process would also help if working on fashion shoots, as what may look good in the flesh may look decidedly frumpy in print.

With male and female celebrity stylists working everywhere from London to New York, Los Angeles, Sydney and beyond, the good news is that this career is open to any enterprising fashion junkie who is willing to work hard to build a profile for themselves. No need for a college education – you can swat up on trends yourself by reading widely, attending fashion shows or working for a fashion magazine or within a boutique.

In this role, you'll be exposed to a fair amount of diva behaviour but you'll also get to attend fashion shows all over the world, work one-on-one with celebrities and receive free handbags, shoes and more. If you're lucky, you'll even get your name dropped on the red carpet (hopefully for all the right reasons).

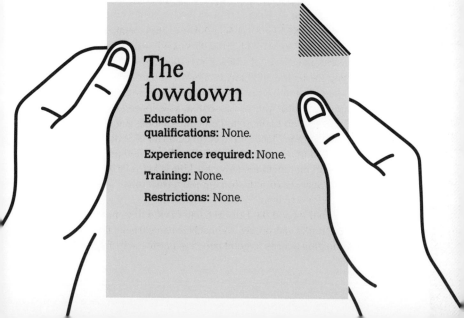

The lowdown

Education or qualifications: None.

Experience required: None.

Training: None.

Restrictions: None.

Certified ethical hacker

The ultimate career move for anyone who has ever been accused of spending too much time 'playing' on their computer, certified ethical hackers work with companies and government organisations to locate weaknesses in their security systems. Also known as 'White Hat Hackers', certified ethical hackers earn a tidy living from putting their hacking talents to good use.

If backdoors, Trojan horses, session hijacking, viruses and worms turn you on, then ethical hacking is a good way to indulge your dark and dirty hacking fantasies while staying on the right side of the law. Using the same skills hackers use to commit crimes against corporations, governments and citizens, ethical hackers work to identify problems or chinks in the armour of an organisation's digital presence ... hopefully before the bad guys find (and exploit) that very weakness.

Despite the clichéd idea of hackers being anti-social cave dwellers devoid of social skills, this job isn't all about sitting in a dark basement in front of a flickering computer screen. Apart from having the technical ability to identify vulnerabilities in digital security systems, ethical hackers also need soft skills. Being able to communicate with others is essential, as is having the ability to work in a team and adhere to guidelines. Going rogue is not an option in this career. Once you're certified as an ethical hacker, you're expected to understand and follow the guidelines of this profession and that includes never hacking a network without permission. Sorry to ruin the fun but the term 'ethical' is in this career name for a reason.

And now to the good bit. Ethical hackers who have progressed through the ranks and proven themselves can earn six-figure salaries and gain access to good benefits, particularly if working for a government agency or large, multinational corporation. In many ways, ethical hackers get to enjoy the best of both worlds in that they get to use their extensive skills to find weaknesses in security systems, but instead of exploiting that weakness, they help to fix it (and earn a steady income at the same time).

As a thoroughly modern career, ethical hacking may not have mainstream recognition among the masses, but it is a growing sector. And with more and more new viruses and hacking tactics emerging every single day, no two days are the same in this crucial role. Putting your supreme knowledge of information technology (IT) security to good use is a worthy payoff, but getting to tell your friends that you're a professional hacker is even better (and will have them changing their email passwords, pronto).

The lowdown

Education or qualifications: An IT degree or equivalent qualification is commonly required for this role. On top of this, internet security certifications are also required.

Experience required: Experience working in IT security and testing is essential. Programming experience is also useful.

Training: On-the-job training for these types of roles is common, however, hacking knowledge and techniques are often garnered outside of formalised work environments (i.e. your friend's command centre located in their basement).

Restrictions: Some government roles may require criminal record checks and security clearances.

Champagne consultant

Earning a living from drinking Champagne, travelling the world visiting vineyards and attending wine events sure does seem like a job that is too outlandish to even contemplate, but much to everyone else's extreme jealousy, there are people who have carved out a special niche in Champagne consulting.

Benedictine monk Dom Pérignon reportedly exclaimed, 'Come quickly, I am drinking the stars!' during his first taste of Champagne back in 1693 and the world has continued tasting the stars at weddings, engagements and birthdays – and for flamboyant English writer and entertainer Noel Coward, breakfast – ever since.

A sparkling wine produced only from grapes grown in the Champagne region of France, Champagne was a premium alcoholic drink associated with royalty and luxury thanks to a hefty price tag and a history of clever marketing targeted at the ruling classes. These days, Champagne is associated less with the elite and more with celebrations, with bottles of champers being cracked open to toast weddings, smashed over the hulls of new ships, sprayed over winners on the podium of racing events and used to lubricate lips at gallery openings and awards nights.

Combining technical knowledge with wine industry know-how and a dash of showmanship, Champagne consultants live a life full of career variety. From teaching Champagne appreciation courses to judging at international wine events; writing editorials for newspapers, websites and magazines; consulting for Champagne makers (of which there are more than a hundred in France); speaking at wine appreciation events and advising restaurants, bars, hotels and airlines on what bubbles should feature on their menus, Champagne consulting covers a lot of ground. As such, if you want to make it as a Champagne consultant you need to be a pretty special person. Investing many years in tasting Champagne to develop a palate, travelling regularly to the Champagne region in France, forming relationships with winemakers and reading up on the history of Champagne may sound like a gloriously fun folly to be involved in, but in the world of Champagne it takes years to rise to the top and become known and regarded as an expert.

French language skills, while not essential, will help you greatly, as will the ability to market yourself and network with everyone from wine experts to the lifestyle media. Without possessing a sincere, true love for Champagne this career would be sheer hell, as consultants live and breathe their work – constantly tasting, writing and talking about Champagne.

For anyone with a taste for the good life, this is truly a dream job. Being paid to taste Champagne, have influence over the wine industry, work with everyone from restaurateurs to the world's greatest winemakers, and have access to some of the rarest (and tastiest) tipples in the world rates as a 'pinch me' career move worth celebrating. So, santé!

The lowdown

Education or qualifications: None.

Experience required:
Well-rounded knowledge of the Champagne industry, usually gathered during years of tasting, learning, reading and attending wine events and shows.

Training: Most Champagne experts are self-taught, or learn by apprenticing with senior winemakers or Champagne experts.

Restrictions: Must be able to drink alcohol, have fully functioning taste buds and a good sense of smell.

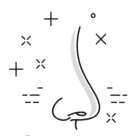

Chief sniffer

Here's a career straight from the 'this cannot be true' files: there are people in this world employed to smell things. All day long they put their nose to work in order to make the world a better place. If you've got a nose for detecting odours and want to avoid following a run-of-the-mill career path, then aim for the ultimate sniffing role: Chief Sniffer at NASA.

Yes, you read that right. NASA has employed a full-time smeller for the past forty years. Tasked with smelling a range of items that will end up in space, NASA's chief sniffer uses their smelling superpowers to ensure that no toxic, flammable items accidently end up in orbit where they could threaten the safety of a mission. Giving everything from toothpaste to fabric and electrical equipment the smell test, it's not a stretch to say that the work of the chief sniffer is actually a matter of life and death.

Of course, all items are put through a series of other tests to ascertain toxicity levels and avoid space fatalities, and the smell test is a part of the process. Safety is a huge reason sniffers are employed by NASA, but another important factor is comfort. Can you imagine doing a long stint at the International Space Station and being trapped with an awful odour the whole time? Astronauts need to protect their mental health, and there is nothing worse than having to live and work in a confined space with a funky stench following your every move.

The chief sniffer heads up a team of extreme sniffers working in the Molecular Desorption and Analysis Laboratory. Their job is to ensure that astronauts are safe and comfortable when in space. With everyday items smelling different in different atmospheres, the sniffers have fine-tuned their noses to detect odours that just don't work in space. By scaling and rating all items on the panel, sniffers are able to put forward recommendations for which items should and shouldn't go into orbit.

While you may be having a laugh at this career, it's actually a serious job, with all sniffers having to complete a sniff test every few months to ensure that their senses are performing to the standards needed at NASA. Imagine failing a sniff test? The humiliation! In the case that a sniffer fails the test repeatedly, they are pulled out of the team and replaced with someone else. And no, dogs can't perform this role. Dogs are known to have a very keen sense of smell, but they have a different palate that is better used for detection (not grading).

As far as finances go, this is a full-time job at one of the world's leading space agencies, so it's pretty well paid. A degree isn't necessary, but freakish smelling ability is. If you're always asking 'what's that smell?' then this might be the career for you.

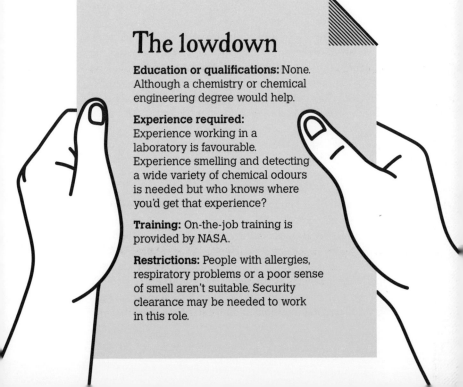

The lowdown

Education or qualifications: None. Although a chemistry or chemical engineering degree would help.

Experience required: Experience working in a laboratory is favourable. Experience smelling and detecting a wide variety of chemical odours is needed but who knows where you'd get that experience?

Training: On-the-job training is provided by NASA.

Restrictions: People with allergies, respiratory problems or a poor sense of smell aren't suitable. Security clearance may be needed to work in this role.

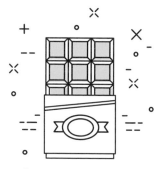

Chocolatier

If I told you there was a career that involved contributing to the happiness levels of the world *and* it involved having access to free chocolate, you'd think I'd just regurgitated the plot of Roald Dahl's *Charlie and the Chocolate Factory* and passed it off as fact. But in reality, there are many Willy Wonkas working all around the world, creating handmade chocolate treats that instantly make the world that little bit sweeter. They are the chocolatiers that give children sugar rushes, make diabetics sad and keep dentists in business.

When I write of the chocolatier profession, I'm not referring to working at the Cadbury factory (although that sounds alright too). When I refer to chocolatiers, I mean highly skilled people who are dedicated to hand-crafting chocolate delights, à la the character played by Juliette Binoche in *Chocolat*. Of course, there's always a place for mass-produced chocolates at the dessert buffet but, as a career choice, becoming an independent chocolatier is very different from a shift monitoring the Cadbury Crème Egg machine at the factory.

Chocolatiers usually start out as pastry or confectionery chefs, then work their way into the chocolate scene, although this isn't always the case. While chocolate might seem a simple thing to eat, it's a very challenging food to work with. As such, many years are invested in learning the techniques needed to make successful sweet treats. From learning about cacao percentages to becoming an expert in the art of tempering and having a good understanding of food safety, becoming a skilled chocolatier is no easy feat.

Becoming a chocolatier is possible almost anywhere and in some parts of the world it's easier than others, with France, Belgium, Switzerland, Mexico and eastern Canada all having very vibrant chocolate-making traditions. Some cities have chocolate-making schools. Canada's Ecole Chocolat school is well regarded, while the Chocolate Academy has locations everywhere from Singapore to Spain, Chicago and Moscow.

Most chocolatiers tend to run their own businesses, crafting chocolates for the masses or producing bespoke chocolate delights for events such as weddings. Some choose to work in high-end restaurants, six-star cruise ships and luxury hotels. Regardless, the ultimate endgame that most chocolatiers aspire to is becoming known as a master chocolatier. Considered the best of the very best, master chocolatiers compete at the World Chocolate Masters each year. Imagine being a judge at that event!

Combining sheer culinary talent with creative flair, chocolatiers may be working in a job that has existed for centuries, but the need to innovate is still present. As such, a successful chocolatier must have an eye on current food trends and the ability to consistently bring new flavours, designs and creations to the table. In short, you really do need to be like Willy Wonka (without exploiting an army of orange, short-statured people, of course).

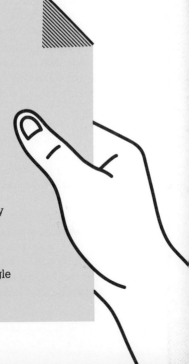

The lowdown

Education or qualifications: No formal educational requirements.

Experience required: Many years working as a pastry chef or confectionery maker are needed before stepping into the role of a chocolatier.

Training: On-the-job training by apprenticing under another pastry chef or chocolatier is common, as is attending culinary school or a chocolate academy.

Restrictions: Diabetics will struggle with this profession.

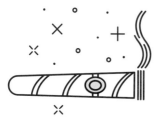

Cigar sommelier

If you love nothing more than lighting up a stogie, as Winston Churchill did, then you'll be pleased to know that your cigar-loving ways don't just have to be relegated to hobby status for life. Oh yes, it's entirely possible to build a whole career out of sharing your cigar knowledge and, while it's considered a niche profession, someone's got to do it and that someone might as well be you.

Cigar sommeliers are cigar-tasting experts sometimes also known as catadors. Although most of us have heard of wine sommeliers, cigar sommeliers tend to fly under the radar for a number of reasons. Blame the anti-smoking movement, blame the increase in knowledge about the ill effects of cigar smoking, blame the lingering odour that comes with cigars – whichever way you look at it, cigars aren't as popular as they used to be. And it's for this reason that cigar sommeliers aren't as well known as wine sommeliers.

Working with hotels, restaurants, high-end cruise ships and casinos, cigar producers and sellers, and the media, cigar sommeliers work hard to inform and educate others on the joys of smoking cigars. They put together cigar menus for luxury hotels and bars; write articles on cigar trends for magazines, newspapers and websites; teach cigar tasting in workshops; and sit on cigar-tasting panels at cigar awards shows. Cigar sommeliers live and, quite literally, breathe their work.

Not convinced that cigar sommeliers are needed in this world? Well, just like a fine wine, cigars have flavour notes. Yes, beyond that strong initial taste, there are subtle flavours to be detected – from moss to tea, molasses, cherry, caramel, leather, honey and beyond. As cigar-smoking newbies gag at their first puff, discerning cigar lovers can detect different flavours.

A cigar sommelier must demonstrate in-depth knowledge of the cigar industry, from the production process to tobacco growing. A good cigar sommelier will also know about dining and food trends, in order to put together top-notch cigar menus for restaurants (yes, cigars can be matched to food and wine).

If you don't know how to cut and light a cigar properly, then you're definitely not the right calibre to pull this career off. The best cigar sommeliers in the world are discerning, thorough and utterly obsessed with cigars.

If you make it to the top of this career, then you'll get to enjoy frequent travel and visits to world-class hotels, luxe bars and high-end restaurants. In all likelihood, you'll also get to rub shoulders with everyone from tobacco growers in South America to expert rollers in Cuba and billionaires in the Middle East. And you'll get unlimited access to the best cigars in the world. This is one smokin' hot career.

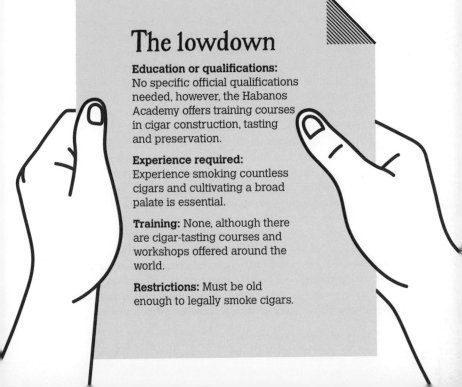

The lowdown

Education or qualifications:
No specific official qualifications needed, however, the Habanos Academy offers training courses in cigar construction, tasting and preservation.

Experience required:
Experience smoking countless cigars and cultivating a broad palate is essential.

Training: None, although there are cigar-tasting courses and workshops offered around the world.

Restrictions: Must be old enough to legally smoke cigars.

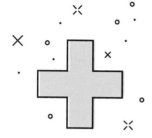

Clown doctor

Want to help heal sick people but didn't get the astronomical grades required to study medicine? Do you love the idea of working in a hospital but don't feel comfortable wielding a scalpel or hypodermic needle? The people in hospitals and health facilities who are battling illness, injury and the cruel ravages of time need more than a doctor – they need *lots* of comic relief. And that is where clown doctors enter, stage left.

Popularised by the loveable character played by Robin Williams in *Patch Adams*, being a clown doctor is a real profession pursued by performance artists all around the world. Sometimes referred to as 'clown care', specialised clown performers are employed everywhere from children's hospitals to aged care facilities and palliative care wards. Working hard to reduce the trauma that comes with being hospitalised, clown doctors have been known to play a pivotal role in the recovery of patients.

Walking the wards entertaining patients as they go, clown doctors are capable of doing everything from making chemotherapy treatment less daunting for cancer patients to demystifying all the frightening hospital machinery and contraptions that scare children (CT scanner, we're looking at you). Lightening the emotional load for patients, families and medical staff, clown doctors inject some good old-fashioned fun into a decidedly un-fun situation.

Despite appearances, the red noses and goofy, giant shoes of clown doctors aren't just a feel-good exercise. Pioneered in a New York hospital in the 1980s, clown care has been proven to have real benefits and has now spread to hospitals and aged care facilities all over the world. With humour proven to boost immunity, reduce stress and release feel-good hormones, laughter really is some of the best medicine going around. Recognising this, many institutions are including clown care within their frameworks. Only recently, Argentina passed a law making clown doctors a mandatory fixture within all public hospitals in Buenos Aires.

When it comes to creativity, this career choice is off the hook. Clown doctors have to use their imagination and think on their feet every single day. Stepping into an alternative persona every time they put on their oversized floppy shoes, clown doctors are magicians, stand-up comedians, storytellers, dancers, vaudeville performers and more. When it comes to forging a career with meaning, this job delivers bonus points in spades. Being able to positively influence the recovery of a patient with nothing more than a gag and a smile is something truly special. Sure, clown doctors experience heartbreak when patients can't be cured and families are lost in grief, but the emotional rewards of this job are immense. Plus, you get to say you're a clown doctor.

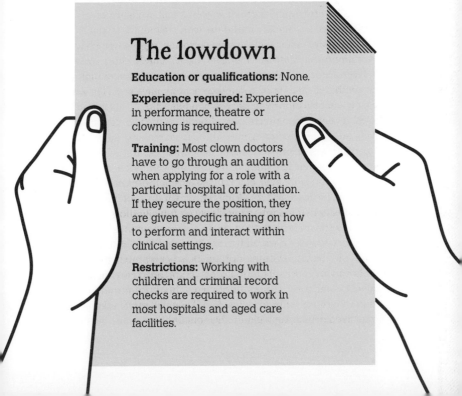

The lowdown

Education or qualifications: None.

Experience required: Experience in performance, theatre or clowning is required.

Training: Most clown doctors have to go through an audition when applying for a role with a particular hospital or foundation. If they secure the position, they are given specific training on how to perform and interact within clinical settings.

Restrictions: Working with children and criminal record checks are required to work in most hospitals and aged care facilities.

Cocktail writer

Getting paid to drink cocktails is surely the ultimate boss career move. Only a handful of people have ever been able to pull it off, but don't let that stop you. If you love getting stuck into a Manhattan or would walk ten city blocks for the best mojito in town, then the life of a cocktail writer might be for you. If you manage to be one of the few who crack it in this highly competitive writing niche, a fascinating, fun and super-indulgent career awaits.

Cocktail writers are employed by magazines, newspapers, websites and other publishers to stay on top of the latest in cocktail trends. Commonly based in large, cosmopolitan (pardon the cocktail pun) cities with thriving foodie scenes – places like, but not limited to, London, New York, Los Angeles, Paris, Sydney and Berlin – cocktail writers are paid to go to bars, restaurants, clubs and hotels and write about the cocktail offerings. They also interview people involved in the scene – bar tenders, spirit makers and restaurant owners – and attend cocktail-making competitions, shows and other industry events.

But while this career is certainly big on indulgence – cocktail writers attend their fair share of parties and launches – there is actual work and skill involved in this profession. You have to know your stuff. If you can't tell the difference between a gin or vodka martini, then you're useless. And if you don't know the perfect Negroni when you taste it, then you're also unsuitable for the job. It could be argued that cocktail writers have more in-depth knowledge of their field than most other journalists, so expect to invest many, many hours in drinking before you can be considered an expert (read up on hangover cures while you're at it). Furthermore, if you don't have writing skills, forget it. And if you just aren't all that into spirits-based drinks, then get the hell out of here.

Just like other writers, cocktail reviewers must meet deadlines, be able to draw interesting information and juicy quotes from their interview subjects, and have enough creative flair to produce entertaining, enthralling content day in, day out (although, how could writing about cocktails ever get old?). They also have to possess a keen eye for trends and be able to discern between a flash-in-the-pan fad and a more enduring contribution to the cocktail scene.

Most cocktail writers write for the media on a freelance basis, so job security can be a concern for some. When you consider that cocktail-focused stories can be found everywhere from in-flight magazines to national newspapers, blogs and lifestyle websites, it's clear the opportunities are there if you're clever enough to network with editors and regularly pitch on-trend story ideas. Some writers who specialise in cocktails have gone on to write books – either guides to cocktail making (and drinking) or more detailed tomes on the history and culture of the cocktail. The point is: cocktail drinking *can* be turned into a career. Cheers to that!

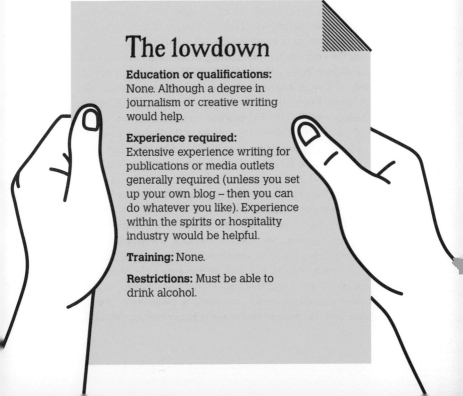

The lowdown

Education or qualifications:
None. Although a degree in journalism or creative writing would help.

Experience required:
Extensive experience writing for publications or media outlets generally required (unless you set up your own blog – then you can do whatever you like). Experience within the spirits or hospitality industry would be helpful.

Training: None.

Restrictions: Must be able to drink alcohol.

Comedian

Class clowns unite! There is a way to turn your formidable talents for making others laugh (and teachers cry) into something more than a week-long stint in detention. You'll be pleased to know that there's a ragtag bunch of people scattered around the world making money from making people laugh. And you can be one too!

Comedians have existed in many different forms for eons. Whatever is happening in the world, god knows people need to laugh. Come to think of it, most of the people need to laugh *because* of what's happening the world. Much more than just entertainers, comedians shed light on important social issues, lampooning everything from crooked governments to billionaires who don't pay tax.

From the edgy social commentary of Richard Pryor to the sharp tongue of Joan Rivers, the satire of Bill Hicks and the physical comedy of Rowan Atkinson playing Mr Bean, comedians take many forms. But while it may appear to be a fun-filled, light-hearted profession, anyone who has worked in comedy knows the dark side of this creative career. The cliché of the sad clown often rings true, with many comedians using their platform to exorcise their personal demons. Whether those demons are drug abuse, chronic anxiety or a full-blown personality disorder, comedians often lay themselves bare on stage and screen, and often cop a fair amount of criticism in the process.

Aaaah yes, all stand-up comedians know that at some moment in their career they will have to bomb on stage. It's obvious that a knack for comedy is needed to become a working comedian, but being brave, accepting knockbacks and stepping up to the plate after failure are arguably more important than having raw comedic skill. If you're thin-skinned and lack confidence, you'll be unable to deal with the hecklers and bad reviews that come with performing comedy.

But stand-up performance is only one element of comedy. Many comedians also work as MCs for corporate gigs, write their own books, act in films, and work as comedy writers for television shows. Many comedians, except maybe Jerry Seinfeld and Chris Rock, admit that their finances are in a perpetual state of disarray, but there are plenty of ways for enterprising comedians to make money if they are prepared to work hard and hustle.

Financial insecurity and public ridicule aside, comedy can provide a steady stream of career riches in the form of travelling the world to perform at comedy festivals and clubs, having audiences in the palm of your hand, and bringing bucketloads of joy to people in need of a good gut-busting laugh. With laughter scientifically proven to decrease stress hormones and increase production of immune cells, it wouldn't be a stretch to say that comedians are healing the world, one dirty joke at a time.

Word of warning though: This is one of those professions that will have teachers, parents, guidance counsellors and other straight-laced dream crushers turning up their noses. Best to start early and have an arsenal of zingers to slay them with, because you really can't criticise someone else if you've wet your pants with laughter.

The lowdown

Education or qualifications: None required. Some comedians have degrees in performance arts.

Experience required: None. Although you should get better as you go along.

Training: None. Some comedians attend performance workshops but it's not always necessary.

Restrictions: None

Composer

Here's one career suited to musical geniuses, prodigies and fanatics. If you can think of nothing better than spending your days tinkering away in a music studio chasing the best combination of sounds to elicit emotional responses from audiences, then the life of a composer may be for you.

Hans Zimmer. Leonard Bernstein. John Cage. Brian Eno. Modern composers like these shape the viewing experience. They provide original music for movie soundtracks, ceremonies, commercials, television series, musicals, operas and other live performances. Composers interpret scripts, treatments and creative briefs to then set the mood for a performance, event or piece of filmed work.

Although the likes of Brahms, Handel and Beethoven are gone, modern composers still have plenty of influence over the world, albeit in markedly different ways from their classical counterparts. From the chilling music of Alfred Hitchcock's *Psycho* to the unforgettable score of *Jaws* and the tear-jerking soundtrack to *Cinema Paradiso*, creating memorable, moving soundtracks is the task of many modern composers.

A variety of musical skills and knowledge is needed to build a career as a composer. Apart from being able to play at least one instrument and read sheet music, composers must have an inherent understanding of the medium they are creating music for; so if you want to compose for film and television you need to know the business. Having the vision and depth to be able to interpret a script and create music to suit the themes and moods is essential, so is the ability to liaise and communicate with directors, musicians and producers.

While top-level composers can earn high amounts of money, it's still a niche profession where only a few reach the dizzying heights of the Academy Awards and Grammys. As such, to carve out a career in composing means you have to love music more than you love life itself (because there will be hard times, especially when you're starting out and are relatively unknown).

The best bet for anyone wanting to become a composer is to listen to a wide variety of music, study the craft at a tertiary level or at a music school, pick up as many instruments as you can and really study the medium you want to compose for. As a highly competitive career, composing jobs aren't exactly a dime a dozen, so being persistent and determined are necessary qualities to make it.

There may be lean times and frustrations, such as dealing with wishy-washy studios that cancel projects at a moment's notice, but there are also plenty of positives to composing. You could end up working with the greatest artists and musicians in the world. You could end up writing an award-winning score. You could even be responsible for creating a cult horror flick score that strikes fear into the heart of viewers for decades to come. Quite an accomplishment, huh?

The lowdown

Education or qualifications: None officially required but tertiary qualifications in music are helpful.

Experience required: Experience working with orchestras and musicians is essential, as is having written original pieces of music. Composers must know their way around studios and have experience in operating recording studio equipment.

Training: Having trained in a particular musical instrument is essential, as is having been instructed in building scores and writing sheet music. It doesn't matter if this training comes from an Ivy League College, a community college or in a more informal setting.

Restrictions: None.

Conductor

Ever looked at that tuxedo-wearing person standing in front of an orchestra with a tiny baton and thought it looked like a pretty cool job? Well, despite being quite a niche profession, conducting is a genuine career path if you possess the perfect storm of skills and temperament needed to lead an orchestra to musical glory.

Most conductors start out playing an instrument in an orchestra before giving it up to pursue conducting. Sometimes also known as musical directors or maestros, conductors must have the ability to read sheet music, comprehend all the terminology used for musical performances, and have a thorough understanding of all the instruments that make up an orchestra. Foreign language skills are also useful when trying to understand the terminology and converse with musicians from a wide range of backgrounds. Possessing crazy hair and a bit of eccentric flair seems to be helpful, but isn't a prerequisite.

Some naysayers believe that conductors aren't necessary, however, conductors work to bring the very best out of the orchestra, elevating their performance to higher levels. Most orchestras and musical ensembles still elect to have a conductor to help the musicians work together seamlessly. And who would the audience look at without having a flailing-armed figure furiously whipping up energy at the front?

As figureheads, conductors are ultimately responsible for the performance of an orchestra, so they need to be able to perform under pressure and work through problems without losing the plot. Any conductor who has invested the time to perfect the skills needed to successfully lead an orchestra will be rewarded with a juicy musical career full of life, colour and inspiration. Given the chance to work with some of the world's best musicians, in some of the world's greatest auditoriums, this exciting career combines two of greatest reasons to live: music and travel. If that's music to your ears, you better start keeping time.

The lowdown

Education or qualifications: Although not essential, many conductors have degrees in the arts, music or music education fields.

Experience required: Extensive experience working with orchestras and musicians is essential.

Training: Many conductors learn the art through musical training of their own. Some graduate school programs offer training in the art of conducting.

Restrictions: Must be able to read sheet music.

Contortionist

If you're able to entertain your friends with your freaky levels of flexibility, then there could be a way to make a career out of your party trick by becoming a professional contortionist. In this career choice, you could find yourself suspended up in the air from a rope in front of thousands of audience members or squeezing yourself into a tiny glass box for a television commercial. Either way, you'll have a career that never fails to amaze people.

Stretching, bending and squishing themselves into unthinkable poses, contortionists perform in dance troupes, theatre productions, circuses, large arena shows and sometimes as solo acts. Usually starting out in the profession from a young age, contortionists are some of the most hard working, disciplined and resilient entertainers in the business. So if you're lazy, forget it!

Training for up to 5–6 hours a day, or even longer, contortionists follow a very strict lifestyle in order to be able to do what they do. The combination of following a gruelling training regime, strict diet and harsh instruction from trainers means that this career is one of the toughest in the entertainment world. Despite being extremely difficult, contortionists are expected to present their art as completely effortless to an audience. Not only do contortionists have to pull off near-impossible physical feats, they have to do it without sweating, grimacing or grunting. So they're basically superheroes in leotards.

The physical demands of being a contortionist are obviously significant but there are other skills needed for a successful career in this oh-so-tricky performance art. Having a good understanding of crowd dynamics and the entertainment industry helps, as does having the confidence to market yourself to agents, bookers and theatre companies. Coming from a ballet or gymnastics background is helpful, not only with flexibility but with developing the patience and resilience needed to perfect complicated manoeuvres and stick to the kind of training schedule most people would abandon in a day.

Injuries are commonplace, with joint pain, dislocations and broken bones all a part of the business. As a contortionist you have to follow a super strict diet, train like a demon, endure physical and mental pain, *and* put up with painful injuries. Why on earth would anyone do it? Well, contortionists often feel like they were born to perform. From performing on the street to shows in large venues around the world, contortionism can be a fun, lucrative career – especially if you land a job with a prestigious company like Cirque du Soleil.

Travelling around the world performing everywhere from Las Vegas to Paris, Melbourne and Beijing, contortionists manage to get audiences to smile, laugh, gasp and cheer – all by moving their body. Performing in a tight-knit community means that there's a strong sense of solidarity within the sector and even though it's essentially a young person's game, ageing contortionists often transition into teaching or training roles. A highly unusual career choice only suited to a small proportion of the population, contortionism is the ultimate flexible career!

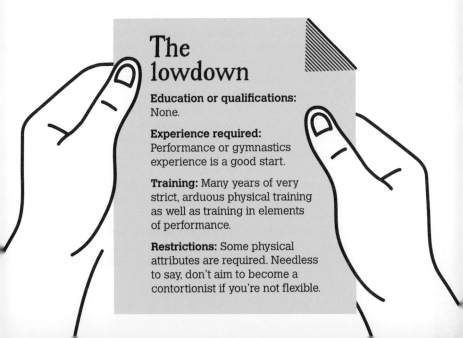

The lowdown

Education or qualifications:
None.

Experience required:
Performance or gymnastics experience is a good start.

Training: Many years of very strict, arduous physical training as well as training in elements of performance.

Restrictions: Some physical attributes are required. Needless to say, don't aim to become a contortionist if you're not flexible.

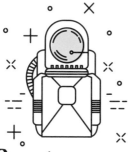

Cosplayer

Listen up! Anyone serious about gaming, anime and comics needs to know that if you're clever you can make money from dressing up as your favourite characters. Professional cosplay is a thing and it's ended up being a wise career move for a few smart operators. From *Game of Thrones* to *Final Fantasy*, *Mortal Kombat* and *Pokémon*, the professional cosplay scene is awash with inspiration. If you're more than a little bit interested in all things *Warcraft*, *Star Wars* and *Halo*, then read on to see how professional cosplayers turn their geekdom into piles of cold hard cash.

While most people tend to get involved in cosplay as a hobby, some have been able to build full-time careers out of dressing up as their favourite anime, superhero and video game characters. Sure, dressing up in elaborate costumes sounds like a walk in the park compared to most jobs, but cosplayers need to work extremely hard to develop enough of a presence in order to generate revenue and sustain a living.

So how do professional cosplayers actually make their dough? If they're savvy enough they can get paid appearance fees to attend geek conventions, associate with brands in ambassadorial roles and model in photoshoots. Smart cosplayers can also set up another income stream by selling merchandise, such as signed photos, to fans and can even sell advertising on their website or social media channels if they have a strong following.

To make all that happen, cosplayers have to invest a lot of time and money into creating next-level looks. From custom-designed leather costumes to wigs, make-up and accessories, cosplay is an expensive game to get into. Then there's the time involved in setting up a cosplay enterprise. With social media being a huge part of professional cosplayers' working lives, many hours must be dedicated to interacting with and updating the fan base that sustains you. This means constantly replying to Facebook messages, uploading new images to Instagram, retweeting key identity tweets and responding to an inbox full of emails.

Taking the above into consideration, the typical professional cosplayer is a savvy businessperson with an inherent understanding of everything from social media to ecommerce, sponsorship deals, contracts and merch sales. And you thought cosplayers just dressed up in cool costumes for a living!

If you're unafraid of hard work, have a genuine love of gaming, comics and pop culture, are able to connect with others and have a strong business sense, then professional cosplaying can open up a world where you get to travel to conventions in places like Tokyo, San Diego and Sydney. You can also earn serious amounts of money if you're lucky enough to hit the big league where six-figure salaries are possible. One hundred grand a year to travel to Japan and hang out with Chewbacca? Yes please!

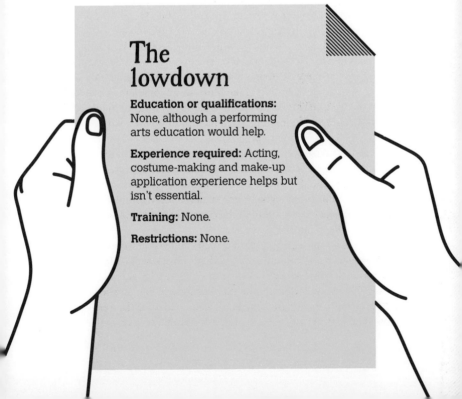

The lowdown

Education or qualifications: None, although a performing arts education would help.

Experience required: Acting, costume-making and make-up application experience helps but isn't essential.

Training: None.

Restrictions: None.

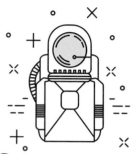

Costume designer

The ultimate career choice for anyone who loved playing dress-ups as a kid or has watched *Marie Antoinette* umpteen times just to swoon over the costumes, costume designing is a highly coveted profession and an integral part of the entertainment industry.

Positions are hotly contested, but costume designers work on television series, films, theatre and ballet productions, advertising campaigns, music videos and live concerts so there is a large variety of work on offer for an enterprising, ambitious designer.

From Marilyn Monroe's show-stopping white dress in *The Seven Year Itch* to Marlon Brando's leather biker ensemble in *The Wild One* and the matching all-white uniforms worn by the storm troopers in *Star Wars* – none of these classic movie moments would have been possible without a talented costume designer. Possessing an intimate understanding of the film's script, plot and characters, costume designers work to create a mood, fulfil a plot theme and further develop a character, and sometimes end up creating an enduring style icon in the process.

Learning to be a costume designer isn't an easy feat, with most costume designers only hitting their stride after decades of study and work within the industry. Some complete tertiary studies, while others apprentice under senior designers. Many complete unpaid internships just to get a foot in the door, such is the competitive nature of the business.

Apart from having the technical skills and vision to be able to sketch and create costumes, the ability to work well with others is paramount, as most costumes are designed and made in teams. While having creative flair and possessing drawing and sewing skills is a given, costume designers also need to be thoroughly practical in order to deliver within a certain timeframe and budget.

Having a good understanding of the functionality of the costumes you work on is also of great importance, as there is no point creating an elaborate, period-era costume if it restricts the actors from moving freely on the stage or set.

One of the hardest working teams on set, costume designers don't just fluff around with pretty clothes. Working ridiculously long hours for weeks or months on end, costume designers are expected to be flexible, available and willing to solve problems and update wardrobes at a moment's notice.

Despite the long hours and stresses that come with working in the entertainment industry, costume design can lead to the most incredible places – from the West End of London to New York's Broadway, the back lots of Hollywood or the Sydney Opera House. You just might find yourself up on stage accepting an Academy Award. Better start writing your acceptance speech now.

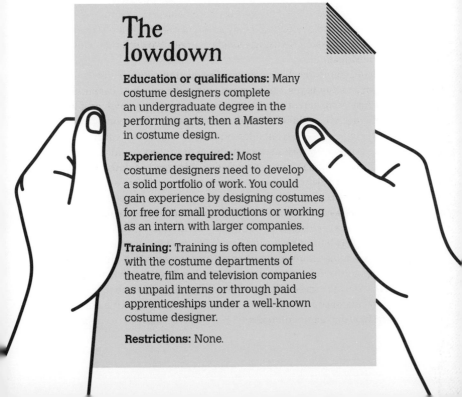

The lowdown

Education or qualifications: Many costume designers complete an undergraduate degree in the performing arts, then a Masters in costume design.

Experience required: Most costume designers need to develop a solid portfolio of work. You could gain experience by designing costumes for free for small productions or working as an intern with larger companies.

Training: Training is often completed with the costume departments of theatre, film and television companies as unpaid interns or through paid apprenticeships under a well-known costume designer.

Restrictions: None.

Court sketch artist

If you're a skilled illustrator with a talent for pulling off sketches of others, who loves nothing more than to tune into an episode or two of *Judge Judy*, then think about combining both of those passions to create a quirky career fusion like no other. Law + illustration = court sketch art. And for some people, that's the career of their dreams.

With the ability to capture the human form using pencils and crayons, court sketch artists document legal trials through the art of sketching. Not affiliated with the legal system, court sketch artists are usually freelance illustrators who are hired by newspapers and other media outlets to cover a trial or supply sketches on a per-piece basis. Some court sketches artists even sell their work to individuals.

Wait ... don't they have cameras in courtrooms now? The answer to that is yes and no. Some jurisdictions allow cameras in courtrooms but others do not. Some cases are so high profile that judges ban all recording devices from the courtroom. Court sketching has been around for centuries – the Salem witch trials were sketched by artists back in the 17th century – and while cameras and video cameras have definitely made a dent in this career, court sketch artists are still hired around the world on a regular basis.

Television dramas like *Law & Order* would have you believe that court cases are dramatic, enthralling affairs. In reality, most cases are terribly boring, so having the ability to sit still for long periods of time is important, as court cases can often drag on for months. Being able to focus on the task at hand and not get distracted is also essential, as is having the strength to sketch through disturbing moments of testimony like seeing photos of bloody crime scenes and hearing about autopsies.

Like many freelance art careers, making enough money can be a serious challenge in this job. That is why many court sketch artists also take on other illustration jobs. It's such a narrow field that it pays to be open to other illustrating work when it comes up. Promoting your work is a huge part of this role, so having the confidence to market yourself and sell your sketches to news outlets is vital.

Typically working on high-profile trials, this career represents a golden opportunity to be involved in something the whole world is watching. With sketch artists capturing iconic moments involving everyone from Charles Manson to OJ Simpson, court sketch work is a rare chance to not only be a part of history, but also shape the way people view a historic event.

If you've got the ability to think quickly, turn sketches around fast enough to feed the news cycle and are okay with hearing the graphic details, then courtroom sketching could provide the perfect outlet for your creative talents and fascination for true crime. You may not get to meet Judge Judy, but your work could end up on the front page of *The New York Times*.

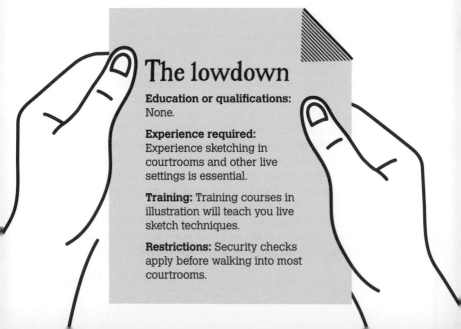

The lowdown

Education or qualifications: None.

Experience required: Experience sketching in courtrooms and other live settings is essential.

Training: Training courses in illustration will teach you live sketch techniques.

Restrictions: Security checks apply before walking into most courtrooms.

Craft beer historian

It seems almost unfair to include this one-in-a-million career in this book but in the spirit of having a good look at what career options are out there, it would be remiss to overlook the role of a craft beer historian. So activate your emergency anti-envy shield; we're about to dive into the heady world of craft beer history.

While the rest of the academic world was spending time studying plants under microscopes or writing papers on economic theory, some genius individual was dedicating their life to learning everything about the history of craft beer brewing and drinking.

Proving that studying hard and following your passions does pay off for some, this individual is now employed at the Smithsonian's National Museum of American History. Tasked with the considerable job of documenting the history of brewing, craft brewers and the beer industry in the United States of America, this is a seriously mammoth undertaking. Needless to say, more skills than being able to neck an IPA in a minute are needed to pull this off.

As a research-based academic role, a craft beer historian needs to have completed a degree in modern history, with some sort of focus on beer included within that study. They should have a sound understanding of the research techniques needed to curate a historical collection. Good writing skills would also help, as reading and writing is a huge part of this role (no, you don't get to sip pilsners in cool microbreweries all day). Having curatorial experience or knowledge is helpful, as ultimately the research findings need to be shared with scholars and the beer-loving public.

Working on documenting everything from early brewing techniques to the lives of the people who work in brewing, this role involves locating and wading through historical records and photographs, interviewing influential figures in the brewing industry, and yes, visiting a fair few breweries too. Essentially, every working day is spent immersed in beer (well, not literally) so you'd have to be comfortable reading, talking and writing about beer and ultimately, living and breathing all things beer.

If this sounds like the job of your dreams, you're not alone. And this is the cruel part ... at the moment there can be only one craft beer historian. This isn't the type of job you could pick up easily after completing your history degree. It may be a unicorn role, but don't you feel better just knowing that it exists?

The chances of landing a killer role like this are exceedingly slim. Nevertheless, next time you're in a bar cracking open a cold one, don't forget to raise your glass to the person employed to specialise in craft beer history. The lucky devil is living the dream of every craft beer lover and, who knows, they may be paving the way for more beer history roles in the future. One can only dream ...

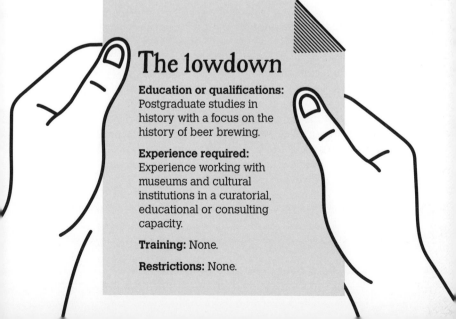

The lowdown

Education or qualifications:
Postgraduate studies in history with a focus on the history of beer brewing.

Experience required:
Experience working with museums and cultural institutions in a curatorial, educational or consulting capacity.

Training: None.

Restrictions: None.

Creative coach

One of the best ways to tackle being unemployed is to give yourself a job. Yes, that's right. Just go right ahead and make up your own job title, buy yourself a desk or rent an office, then get out there and market yourself to people. Many people do this – especially people who look through job ads and observe traditional career paths and see nothing worth pursuing. Many creative coaches can be put in this basket. Instead of wallowing in pity about how the job market is screwed and all 'work' is pointless, they use their creativity to fashion themselves a career in creative coaching.

The work of a creative coach is similar to that of a life coach, but with a strong focus on the creative side of life. Running their own enterprises, creative coaches consult with groups and individuals who feel they need a bit of a creative boost in their career or workplace. Some creative coaches provide one-on-one coaching to artists, writers, performers and other people working in artistic fields. Others provide creative coaching to businesses that could benefit from using inventive ways of thinking to boost their bottom line and improve staff morale.

Using a variety of techniques and methods, creative coaches aim to change the thinking (and performance) of individuals, groups and organisations that are stuck in a rut. Whether it's a writing exercise designed to unearth fresh ways of thinking or a flashcard game aimed at generating new solutions for old problems, creative coaches inject a breath of fresh air into stale situations.

As a career, creative coaching offers plenty of variety. One day you could be sitting in on a brainstorming session at an advertising agency, and the next you could be working with an author to move past writing blocks in order to finish the novel they've been sitting on for years. Delivering creative thinking workshops to corporations, helping startups find creative solutions to their marketing conundrums, and arranging creative writing programs for organisations with communication problems – creative coaching covers a wide range of tasks.

Like any other person working in a freelance or consulting capacity, the biggest challenges come from getting enough business, especially in the beginning when you're essentially unknown. Many people may not even know what a creative coach is, so you'll need to push up against many boundaries in order to make it.

If you do, then you've got plenty to look forward to. With the ability to chart your own course and steer your own ship, you can market yourself to fill any niche you desire. You don't need a degree for this type of work, so you won't need to invest in many years of study (and crushing student debt) to make it work. All you need is a creative mind, some clever tricks to teach others how to be more creative, the ability to develop a good rapport with a range of people, and the confidence to go out there and convince others that their lives are much better with you in it. And there you have it, your very own job, manufactured, marketed and sold to the masses – by you! Doesn't get much more creative than that.

The lowdown

Education or qualifications: None. Although a degree in arts, fine arts, business or psychology would help.

Experience required: None. Experience working in creative environments would help as would experience in training, counselling, business management or coaching.

Training: None. Although training in personal coaching would help.

Restrictions: None.

Criminal profiler

Think you can outsmart a serial killer? Want to use your powers of deduction to improve the world and keep the community safe? For anyone who has ever watched a crime series or movie thriller and has been fascinated by the world of criminology, the tough but rewarding role of criminal profiler might be of interest.

Working within police units and government agencies, and sometimes working as external consultants brought in for special cases or initiatives, criminal profilers have a very specific skill set. Oh yes, criminal profilers are kryptonite to crooks, as they use their wits and vast reserves of knowledge and experience to pinpoint the personalities, behaviours, motivations and likely next moves of criminals.

Whether it's working on a cold case that has remained unsolved for decades or a fresh series of murders that haunts a community, criminal profilers use a range of skills to put together reports that inform detectives of the type of person who is potentially responsible for the crimes they are investigating. And yes, creativity is a part of the role because thinking outside of the box often leads to breakthroughs in cases.

Apart from being a creative thinker, a typical profiler has a good understanding of criminal psychology and behaviour, garnered from tertiary studies and real-life experience working for (or with) law enforcement and corrections agencies. They understand crime scene protocol, legal frameworks and police terminology. Being able to handle disturbing information and confronting images is an important skill for criminal profilers to cultivate, as this type of role involves working on cases involving sexual predators, kidnappers and murderers. It's nasty stuff to deal with on a daily basis, so criminal profilers need to set aside personal feelings to work on the task at hand.

Despite the long hours and challenging nature of the work, criminal profilers have a job that makes a real, tangible difference to the community. Imagine having the skills to accurately paint a psychological portrait of a criminal that ultimately leads to the capture and arrest of a serial killer. Imagine knowing that your work helps a family finally receive closure after years of sadness and pain. Sure, most cases can't be wrapped up neatly like an episode of *CSI: Miami* and some cases may end up haunting you, but few jobs in this world are as important, or interesting, as this one.

The lowdown

Education or qualifications: Tertiary studies in criminology, criminal justice, behavioural science or forensic psychology are needed.

Experience required: Extensive experience working with law enforcement is essential.

Training: Profiling is included in most criminology and forensic psychology degrees. Law enforcement agencies also train individuals within the department.

Restrictions: Criminal record checks are generally required by most countries and jurisdictions.

Crown jeweller

Being appointed as the crown jeweller for the UK's royal family is one of the rarest opportunities in the world. But don't let that put you off – even though it's an unbelievably prestigious role bestowed on only a handful of people in history, it's important to set your sights high (or just let your mind lapse into a daydream for a little while).

One thing British royalty are known for is their immense collection of highly valuable jewels. But what is one to do with all their jewel-encrusted crowns, diamond brooches, ruby rings and pearl necklaces? And how on earth is one supposed to keep up with all the cleaning and repairs such a collection needs? Well, rest easy knowing that no one in the royal family is staying up late to polish the Queen's precious coronation crown. That's the job of the crown jeweller, and what a mighty job it is.

The type of job only suitable to jewellers with decades of experience in making, repairing and cleaning priceless antique and vintage jewellery, the crown jeweller is appointed by the monarchy to care for the Crown Jewels and the personal jewellery collection of the Buckingham Palace residents, which is valued well into the millions. Travelling to the palace at least once a week, the crown jeweller must ensure that the collection is preserved, clean and safe from damage.

Having access to such a collection is certainly a big deal, so this immense role typically goes to top-tier jewellers with a proud history in this type of work. Apart from having the knowledge and ability to clean, repair and care for antique jewellery, the crown jeweller must have a firm understanding of royal protocol and a good handle on ethics (no you cannot borrow that tiara for the night). Having a careful nature is essential – can you imagine being the person who accidently damages the Crown Jewels?

Gaining regular access to such an intimate part of a monarch's life is a major benefit to this job, as is the well-paying nature of the role. Getting your mitts on some of history's most important items of jewellery is the stuff of dreams. The crown jeweller gets the chance to handle a tiara worn by Queen Elizabeth II or a spoon used by royalty all the way back in the 12th century, much to the envy of every jeweller, history buff and staunch monarchist around the world. This creative career is truly fit for royalty.

The lowdown

Education or qualifications: No degree necessary.

Experience required: Extensive experience in handling, caring for and cleaning antique jewels of high worth.

Training: Anyone who takes up this role is expected to already have all the skills required. Buckingham Palace isn't in the business of running training programs. You must already be the best of the best.

Restrictions: Must be able to live and work near Buckingham Palace. Security clearances also apply.

Cryptographer

Not everyone is suited to the military life, but what if there was a way to help protect your nation and positively serve your country without having to pick up a machine gun or fly a helicopter into a warzone? If you've got well above average mathematical ability, a penchant for code breaking and a love of puzzles, then cryptography might be an interesting career avenue worth pursuing.

A profession most people only encounter when watching nail-biting spy movies, cryptographers aren't just nerdy characters in cyber thrillers; they are an essential part of government agencies and tech companies all over the world. Operating under the radar, cryptographers might not get much international recognition. Nevertheless, their work is indispensable.

Working with organisations to solve crimes, detect threats and protect confidential information, cryptographers work hard to encrypt and decrypt data using a variety of methods. Most cryptographers work with governments, yet some also work with private organisations such as software companies.

Possessing a supreme understanding of complex mathematical theories that would fry the brain of the average person, cryptographers break encryption to decipher coded data, or create encryption to safeguard sensitive data. Apart from having a brain full of mathematical knowledge, cryptographers need to possess analytical skills and an enquiring mind. The possession of high-level tech skills is also required, as most cryptographers work to stop hackers accessing sensitive information online.

So what are the chances of becoming an employed cryptographer? Well, with the explosion of digital data comes the increased need for sophisticated encryption. This is good news for cryptographers because even though the field is small, the number of employed cryptographers is on the rise. A degree in mathematics or information technology is usually required, and very high-level knowledge of algorithms and other methods used in encryption.

Apart from all of the technical and education requirements, cryptographers need to sign confidentiality contracts, have a firm understanding of ethical frameworks and be able to work on complex and challenging projects without cracking under the pressure. Needless to say, if you get angry at unsolved Sudoku puzzles then this isn't the job for you.

The unsung heroes of many a conflict, cryptographers may not have fame or extreme wealth, but their work is highly valuable to the community in a number of ways most people never even think about. If you're okay with being a bit of a dark horse, then cryptography might be for you.

The lowdown

Education or qualifications: A degree in mathematics, information technology or science is needed. Cryptographers also commonly have to pass a series of tests before being qualified for a role.

Experience required: Experience encrypting and decrypting data, past history of working with government agencies and corporations, experience handling sensitive data especially digital data.

Training: Most cryptographers need to pass a series of tests to qualify for roles. Successful applicants receive on-the-job training after being accepted into a program or role.

Restrictions: Background checks and security clearances are usually required so you'll need a clean criminal record.

Custom coffin maker

Working in a career for people who wouldn't be caught dead being buried in a generic metal coffin, custom coffin makers put their artistic ability and building skills to good use by creating one-of-a-kind coffins that inject a sense of fun into funerals. Yes, you did just read the words 'funeral' and 'fun' in the same sentence.

Sure, generic, boring coffins can be bought from funeral homes and even Costco, but what about all the people who don't want to be buried in a chrome box? The personalised casket industry is making its mark on a sector in need of a serious shake-up by providing colourful, quirky coffins that allow a person's personality to come to the party (or funeral).

Gone are the days where funerals were strictly a sombre, black-garbed occasion dominated by religious protocol. Over the years, funerals have evolved to include more colour, more fun and, strangely enough, more life. From people wearing bright colours to getting mourners to break out some dance moves to David Bowie songs, funerals have changed and caskets are no exception.

From shiny hot pink caskets perfect for deceased divas to small but mighty Superman-themed caskets for children who left the earth too soon and sports team-themed coffins for fans who held onto their team to the very end, the custom casket world is bursting with creativity.

Most custom coffin makers work independently in their own businesses, making coffins to order for individuals who want to go out with a bang. Many have background skills in carpentry or other building trades, and have turned to custom coffin making after noticing a gap in the industry or finding a flair for sending people off in style.

While having the practical skills to build coffins is required, coffin makers also need to have the knowledge to be able to adhere to the burial standards and laws set by the country in which they operate. Anyone wanting to grow a career out of coffin making needs to know how to market their services to the public and to funeral homes. As such, understanding marketing and promotional techniques is important. Working one-on-one with grieving families or terminally ill people, being sensitive and empathetic is also important.

This strange little career might not be for everyone, but when considering the ceremonial importance of funerals, and how something as simple as a bright fire-engine red casket can bring a little ray of sunshine to a very sad day, custom coffin making is a good way to make use of your creative skills and make the world a better place, one Trekkie-themed coffin at a time.

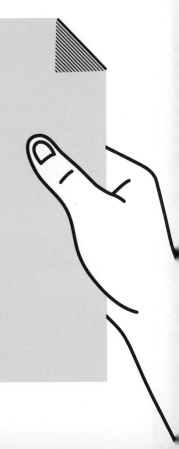

The lowdown

Education or qualifications: No formal education requirements, but degrees in art or design would be helpful.

Experience required: Woodwork or metalwork experience essential. Experience working in the funeral industry would be helpful.

Training: Anyone interested in coffin making should try to apprentice under a custom coffin maker to learn the trade. Woodworking and metalworking courses will also give you the skills needed to craft coffins.

Restrictions: None.

Diplomat

Now here is one of the most misunderstood careers in the world. Think diplomats spend all their time attending black tie dinners full of cigar-smoking cronies? Or that they spend their nights holed up at fancy hotel bars drinking Scotch on the rocks? Or maybe they work really hard to ensure relationships between nations are the best they can be? Read on and you'll find out if the life of a diplomat is all it's cracked up to be, and whether it's for you.

Working on everything from promoting international trade to talking about human rights issues, diplomats work on behalf of their home nation to solidify relationships with the country where they're stationed. Diplomats can end up working anywhere from Paris to Phnom Penh, and while Hollywood would have you believe that all diplomats enjoy luxury hotel stays and access to exclusive events, the reality is somewhat different.

Working in offices and embassies all over the world, diplomats spend most of their time attending meetings with key figures, from local government representatives to heads of NGOs (non-government organisations). Completing reports, emailing contacts and filing updates are large parts of the role so writing skills are essential. Developing strong relationships with locals is a significant component, therefore verbal communication skills are paramount, as is having a good understanding of cultural sensitivity and having … uhh … diplomacy. Working out of hours is very common, as attending events and being on-call to respond to ad hoc things like natural disasters is necessary.

Travel is central to this career, so you'd want to be cool with learning other languages, accepting cultures and customs not your own, and spending a ridiculous amount of time in airport security lines and baggage carousels. If all of that sounds too overwhelming then drop this career idea like a hot potato, as being patient and calm is crucial. Diplomatic disasters can have far-reaching consequences so if you're prone to putting your foot in it or angering quickly, then think about following another path (please ... for the sake of the world).

While quite demanding, the payoffs of this career are plenty – there's the top salary and good benefits, the chance to meet new people, the opportunity to live and work in a variety of places and influence political, economic and social agendas. You also don't need to let your friends know about the more mundane parts of the job, such as filing reports on the local sanitation system – just let them think you're an international woman or man of mystery, then spin some tall stories when you come home for Christmas.

The lowdown

Education or qualifications: Studies in public administration, international development and foreign languages are usually required. The expectations and requirements are different depending on which country you represent.

Experience required: Experience travelling and working in government agencies is helpful. Even experience working at NGOs overseas in a voluntary capacity is helpful.

Training: Most government agencies have their own in-house training program that normally runs for many weeks.

Restrictions: As a government role, criminal record and security checks apply.

Discovery Channel camera operator

Ever watched a Discovery Channel documentary and wondered who the maniac was behind the camera? Blowing the minds of viewers all over the world, the Discovery Channel is responsible for perspective-widening, pulse-quickening, hair-raising documentaries that showcase the best and worst of the natural world. Bringing extreme adventures from around the planet to people sitting safely on their couches, camera operators working in this space certainly earn their salaries.

While competition for all camera-operating roles is tough, competition for this profession is notoriously fierce, with only the most persistent and talented camera operators making the cut. Being hungry for adventure and having extensive experience filming in a wide range of locations are prerequisites for this role. Filming is studios is fine, but if you want to make it as a Discovery Channel camera operator then you need to have really sunk your teeth into projects that include filming outdoors in the elements ... close to terrifying things, such as bears, sharks and ten-foot waves.

Apart from the technical skills that are required to be a camera operator, physical fitness is also essential – you need to be able to operate a camera on location in wild environments. Unlike static studio work, making series and documentaries for the Discovery Channel often involves climbing mountains, hanging off the sides of cliffs, braving the treacherous open oceans and even diving deep into the sea. Having a good understanding of filming during different weather patterns – rain, sleet, snow, fog – is also helpful. Mother Nature is a fickle beast, so you're useless if you freak out when filming in the rain.

Being placed in precarious situations comes with the turf of filming for the Discovery Channel, so having a healthy attitude towards risk-taking (but an even healthier attitude towards safety devices) is needed. Frequent travel to some of the world's most interesting places is a big part of this profession, so being open-minded and culturally aware is essential.

So, while this career involves facing some very challenging physical and mental demands – working in isolated places, completing long climbs, dealing with menacing wildlife – this profession could take you everywhere from the research stations of Antarctica to the deserts of Mongolia, the bear-filled national parks of Canada or the jungles of the Amazon. Camera operators for the Discovery Channel also get to work on documentaries that educate and expand the minds of people all over the world. Best of all, this career has major badass bonus points, perfect for pulling out of the bag when conversations get awkward at high school reunions, family events and first dates. 'What have you done lately?' 'Oh, I've just been in northern India for three months filming the snow leopard in its natural habitat'. Game, set, match: you.

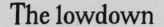

The lowdown

Education or qualifications: None. Although studying journalism, film or media production would help.

Experience required: Experience operating cameras on location in isolated, tough environments is essential. Experience working on documentary projects and short features is also important.

Training: Many camera operators learn the trade while interning at film studios and television production companies. Many start off in the industry as camera assistants before progressing to camera operators.

Restrictions: Must have a valid passport and the ability to travel overseas.

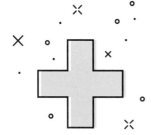

Doll doctor

Do you secretly wish you could still play with dolls like when you were five years old? Well, there's a way you can surround yourself with dolls every day *and* get paid in the process. You may not have the grades to become a medical doctor, but being a doll doctor doesn't require a degree, good grades or the magical ability to not faint at the sight of blood. It just requires a love of dolls, a steady hand and a whole lot of love.

So what on earth does a doll doctor actually do? Well, they don't focus on fixing mass-produced, plastic dolls that you can pick up from the local toy store (when those break they end up in landfill where they will last well beyond the nuclear apocalypse). Instead, doll doctors perform delicate operations on antique dolls, vintage toys and high-value porcelain dolls. Using a variety of techniques, doll doctors know how to repair fine cracks in skulls (sob!), replace broken limbs (arrrrgh) and return a smile to faded lips (yay!).

Despite toys being the focal point of this career, there isn't much time for play. Many dolls are precious family heirlooms, some are valued into the thousands, all are universally loved. As such, repair work is a serious, delicate affair with much at stake, only to be performed by professionals working in doll hospitals. Yes, doll hospitals exist.

Who would make a good doll doctor? Obviously anyone with a pathological fear of dolls is out (I know there are many of you out there). But anyone with skills in repair work would make a good doll doctor. Painting on new faces, repairing ligatures, adhering new wigs to tiny little porcelain heads, doll doctors are part artist, part surgeon, part handyperson, part miracle worker. And although most doll doctors spend their days with lifeless patients, good communication skills are needed to talk with customers and let them know what's possible.

As most doll doctors run their own businesses, they also need to have good skills in finance, record keeping, marketing, customer service and pricing. Working your own hours from your shop, home or studio, you will have an enviable amount of freedom in this career. Doll doctors aren't exactly millionaires, but a solid living can be made if a strong customer base is cultivated.

Perhaps the best part of this job isn't the money earned or the freedom lived but something else, something that can't be quantified by status or dollar symbols. It's that old-fashioned, warm and fuzzy feeling of restoring something with your hands, and thrilling people in the process. Seeing the smile on an elderly person's face when they are reunited with their childhood doll that's been restored to its former glory – that is the stuff that makes getting out of bed worth it. And that is what doll doctors live for.

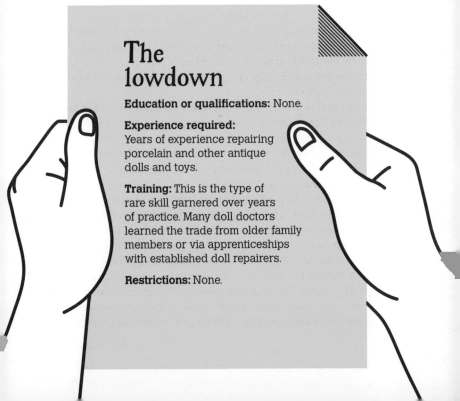

The lowdown

Education or qualifications: None.

Experience required:
Years of experience repairing porcelain and other antique dolls and toys.

Training: This is the type of rare skill garnered over years of practice. Many doll doctors learned the trade from older family members or via apprenticeships with established doll repairers.

Restrictions: None.

Drag queen/king

Do you love to perform to adoring crowds? Are you quick-witted and in possession of a wicked tongue? Have you ever had to declare bankruptcy after a visit to the MAC Cosmetics counter? Well, a career as a drag performer could be for you.

Drag performances (men performing as women on stage) date back to the late 1800s, but it wasn't until the 1970s that drag started to figure more strongly in popular culture. With the growth in awareness of gay rights and the sweeping social change taking place, the barriers that forbade men from dressing as women began to break down. The drag scene finally started to flourish after decades of existing in the shadows, operating in clandestine, dingy bars. By the 1990s drag had well and truly become mainstream, with drag performers appearing everywhere from pubs to work Christmas parties.

Once the domain of (mostly gay) men, drag has evolved of late to include straight men and women. Drag kings (women performing as men) emerged more recently, hitting the scene in the 1990s. Pioneered by New York-based performance artist Johnny Science, drag kings represent a small, yet growing, proportion of the drag scene in comparison to drag queens.

These days, drag is a bona fide art form, way of expression and, for some, a career. While many choose to perform in drag for fun, there are ways to make money from the art of drag. Some choose to perform in venues like clubs and bars, others create their own show and successfully take it on the road. Drag performers are often in demand as MCs or hosts for events. Some people have even carved out careers as drag consultants, offering one-on-one tuition and advice for aspiring drag performers, or more formal courses that run over longer periods – advising on everything from make-up application to how to lip sync better than Britney (which, frankly, isn't too hard).

Encompassing much, much more than putting on a wig and giving yourself a sassy, pun-laden name, drag is an art that takes years to perfect. Not only do performers have to sing, dance and have incredible stage banter with their audience, they also have to know the ins and outs of everything from costuming to theatrical make-up, hair removal and publicity. In drag, only the toughest survive, which is probably why 'I Will Survive' endures as one of the most popular drag anthems.

Successful drag performers are rewarded with legions of fans and a career that can really take them places, from the pubs of outback Australia to the clubs of New York. Best of all, a drag career gives performers the satisfaction that they are spreading joy and bringing colour to an often-grey world. Now there's a good reason to work it, girlfriend!

The lowdown

Education or qualifications: None required, although in 2016 Britain's Edge Hill University became the first in the UK to offer a drag performance module as part of a performing arts degree.

Experience required: None.

Training: Although not a necessity, there are privately owned drag schools, workshops and courses scattered all over the world. Alternatively, any aspiring drag performer worth their salt could learn something from watching every episode of *RuPaul's Drag Race*.

Restrictions: Once the domain of men, the emergence of drag kings ensures women can now also have a slice of the delicious drag pie.

Film critic

While many of us use our downtime to watch movies, some people build a whole career out of it. These people should be applauded because they've managed to find a way to build a life out of watching *Star Wars* (surely the dream of many a teenager in the 1980s).

For anyone with a love of cinema, being a film critic is one of the sweetest gigs in the business. Film critics watch and then review the latest movies – from big budget blockbusters to indie flicks featuring cute, folksy soundtracks, to romantic comedies. Most critics have their written reviews featured in newspapers, magazines and websites, although some have their own television or radio shows or do regular appearances on lifestyle channels. A new wave of self-made reviewers is reaching the world via YouTube.

Getting to watch all the latest releases before they hit the big screens is a perk of the job, but it doesn't end there for many critics. Some get to travel the world to attend movie premieres, awards nights and film festivals. Of course, meeting famous actors, directors and other celebrities is also part and parcel of the life of some critics.

Of course, there's actual talent required to be a critic and plenty of work involved in the reviewing process. Reviews don't write themselves and deadlines don't magically dissolve. Critics not only require a very high level of film production and movie history knowledge, they also need to be able to write entertaining reviews to deadline, or have the charisma and skill to appear on camera if they have a regular television spot. It's safe to say that if you hate writing or appearing in the public eye, then this isn't the career for you. Likewise, if you're not interested in learning the craft of filmmaking. For anyone with a genuine love of film, this should come naturally.

So are there any real downsides to this magical film critic career? Well, this is where the word 'critic' comes in. When your job is to publicly criticise someone else's 'art', then be prepared for some backlash. A thick skin is required to deal with everyone from angry fans to twitter trolls, indignant directors and tortured artists. There's also the fact that you rarely get to select the movies you review, so a lot of your time will be spent sitting through Golden Razzie-worthy stinkers (yes, even late-career Adam Sandler movies need to be critiqued).

Despite having to sit through the odd tired, formulaic bro-comedy and have an awkward moment with a director whose work you've dissed, this is one incredible career for anyone with a love of the silver screen and a way with words.

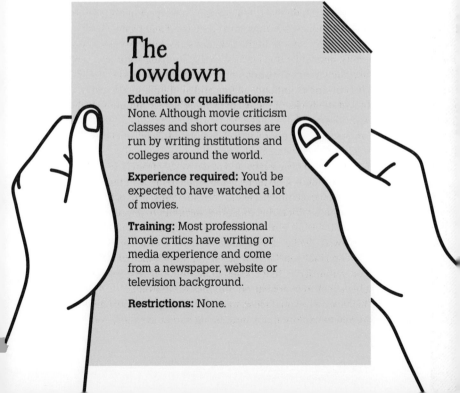

The lowdown

Education or qualifications: None. Although movie criticism classes and short courses are run by writing institutions and colleges around the world.

Experience required: You'd be expected to have watched a lot of movies.

Training: Most professional movie critics have writing or media experience and come from a newspaper, website or television background.

Restrictions: None.

Fine art and antiques appraiser

If you love nothing more than staying in to binge-watch back-to-back episodes of *Antiques Roadshow* while your friends hit the clubs, then perhaps put your passion to work by becoming a fine art and antiques appraiser?

The perfect job for vintage store hounds and lovers of all things from other eras, working as an expert appraiser of fine art and antiques is a solid career choice that could lead to many magical places (the set of *Antiques Roadshow* being just one of them).

There is no magic bullet to becoming an expert in the valuation of art and antiques, but there are some tried and true ways to get there. Many leaders in the field chose to study Art History at university, and while this isn't essential, studying something you love for a few years does sound good. Others rise to the top of the field by working in antiques stores and auction houses, where they are taught the tricks of the trade by more senior antiques dealers and appraisers.

With many expert appraisers choosing to specialise in one particular niche or period of history, this profession allows you to indulge your own obsessions and make money from it. In the world of fine art and antiques, no niche is too small to fill, with many collectors possessing an eccentric mania for certain items, artists or periods in history. From pre-Victorian miniature furniture to jewellery from the Art Nouveau period, antique firearms from the Civil War era and 18th century Swiss clocks, drilling down into one – or a few – specialist areas means that you'll give yourself the best chance at becoming the absolute authority on that chosen item or time period (and a red hot go at being asked to appear on *Antiques Roadshow*).

Whichever way you choose to go, becoming an expert appraiser allows you to explore many interesting career avenues. You can choose to work in a salaried role at a large auction house, such as Christie's, Sotheby's or Bonhams. Or you could set up your own antiques and fine art dealership and enjoy the flexibility and autonomy that comes with running your own business. Alternatively, you could become a consultant and market yourself as a gun-for-hire, available for anything from curating to valuing at fine art fairs, museums and other cultural institutions. Many experts also end up writing books on their specialist subject, lecturing at universities and giving talks at events.

A life immersed in antiques and fine art may sound less than thrilling for some, but this type of work returns very valuable dividends for arts and antiques lovers. Essentially, apart from earning a living, you'll spend your days surrounded by works of rare and immense creativity. From the brushstrokes of Georgia O'Keeffe to the pen of Tolstoy and the detailed craftsmanship of Swiss watchmaker Patek Philippe, this career gives you access to some of the greatest works of art and literature in the world. If your pulse quickens at the thought of handling a signed, first edition copy of *Gone with the Wind* or organising the auction of a Ming vase valued at 53 million dollars, then this is absolutely the life for you.

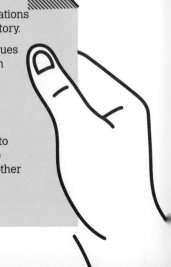

The lowdown

Education or qualifications: Tertiary qualifications in art history are helpful, although not mandatory.

Experience required: Many fine art and antiques experts gain on-the-job experience working in entry-level positions in antiques dealerships, museums and auction houses.

Training: Many fine art institutions, museums and auction houses offer graduate programs and internships for recent graduates looking to enter the industry. Apprenticing under a more experienced antiques or fine art dealer is another way to gain on-the-job training.

Restrictions: None.

Foley artist

If you're gagging to work in the film business but break out in a cold sweat at the very thought of appearing in front of a camera, then a behind-the-scenes role may just be for you. One of the more interesting film roles available in the business, foley artists create sound effects for everything from television ads to Hollywood blockbusters.

Named after Jack Donovan Foley, a pioneer in the early Hollywood sound effects scene, foley artists are employed by television production companies, movie makers and advertising companies. Using a wide range of equipment – surprisingly mostly still very low-fi – foley artists recreate everything from the ominous sound of footsteps chasing a victim in a horror movie, to the gut-wrenching thuds of someone being punched in a fist fight (whoever did the foley work on the Rocky franchise had their work cut out for them).

Even though most of us never think of it, almost every movie and television show includes the important but invisible work of a foley artist. The real-life audio is recorded in the filming, but the quality isn't high enough to reproduce in the final product. Foley artists spend countless days in a studio using all manner of equipment to recreate everyday sounds; they must be inventive problem solvers in order to get the job done. While there are tried and tested tricks to recreating common sounds (for example, a leather bag filled with corn starch makes a noise similar to feet walking through snow), some sounds prove to be difficult to nail, so patience and creativity is needed to get through the trial and error process of recreating elusive sounds.

Working closely with mixers and editors, foley artists need to be able to work as part of a team and have the flexibility to roll with a schedule and script that may change at a moment's notice. As a highly competitive job, being located near cities with large television and film studios would certainly help your career chances, as most of the opportunities are centred in cities like Los Angeles, London and Mumbai (if you're into Bollywood). Needless to say, having the ability to network with producers and directors is crucial. Possessing the confidence to market yourself as the best in the business is key.

This is one of the most overlooked roles in the movie world (don't expect huge amounts of fame, money or recognition to flow your way), but you will be able to contribute to the telling of stories in ways most people wouldn't even dream about. You could be responsible for creating the sound of a blow that ends the life of a major character, or the sound of horse's hooves galloping in to save the day in an Oscar-winning modern classic. All created while playing with everyday items in a studio. Cool career, huh?

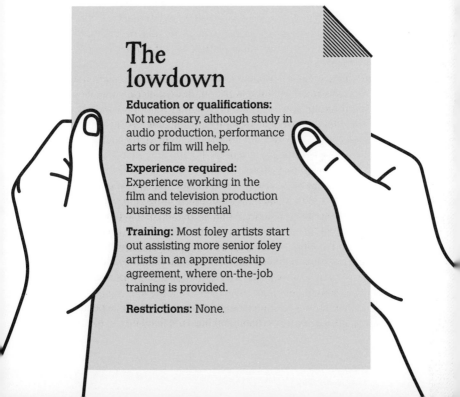

The lowdown

Education or qualifications:
Not necessary, although study in audio production, performance arts or film will help.

Experience required:
Experience working in the film and television production business is essential

Training: Most foley artists start out assisting more senior foley artists in an apprenticeship agreement, where on-the-job training is provided.

Restrictions: None.

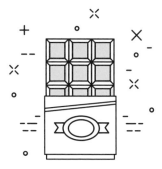

Food stylist

Ever spent hours working on creating a next-level dish you've spotted in a magazine, only to have the end product look nowhere near as delectable as the photo? We've all been there, and we all have food stylists to thank (or curse) for our predicament.

Hired by magazines, newspapers, cookbook publishers, restaurateurs and food marketing companies, food stylists do exactly what their job titles suggest – they style food for photoshoots. Just as fashion stylists put together killer outfits that make fashionistas scream: 'Shut up and take my money', food stylists create the ultimate plate of food that makes people want whatever is on the plate.

Working with recipe developers, editorial staff, photographers and directors, food stylists can be found working on photoshoots and television commercial shoots. Whether they are working on the next must-have cookbook, a single magazine feature, or a marketing campaign for a grocery giant, food stylists are in demand across the publishing and marketing sectors.

While this may seem like a dream job for food lovers, the life of a food stylist is far more complicated than it appears on the surface. For starters, food stylists don't sit around eating all day. They don't even eat the plate of food they've styled, mainly because any plate of food photographed for commercial or editorial purposes is rendered completely inedible by the styling process. In order to create 'the perfect plate' the food is manipulated, rearranged, poked, prodded and pushed to the point where anyone working on the photoshoot would have to be paid to eat the damn thing (even if they were starving). Angel hair pasta is sprayed with hairspray to give it a glossy sheen, cardboard is inserted between burger layers to ensure structural integrity, and cocktails are filled not with ice cubes but plastic faux cubes that never melt.

This may paint a rather unglamorous picture of the profession, yet there are many rewards that come with being a food stylist. Most food stylists are freelancers, meaning they have the freedom and flexibility to work on whatever projects come their way. Furthermore, this type of work involves collaboration with many other creative minds – food stylists rub shoulders with everyone from photographers to celebrity chefs, book publishers and editors. Some food stylists can express their creativity in the most wondrous of ways, with some recipe books featuring plates that look like a work of art. And finally, they get the pleasure of knowing their work is reaching thousands, if not millions of people. Millions? Well, next time you look up at a fast food menu and order the burger you know won't look anything like it does on the menu, just remember that a food stylist was paid to use tweezers to place individual sesame seeds on that glistening burger bun. And that too could be you!

The lowdown

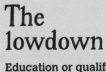

Education or qualifications: No formal education requirements are required.

Experience required: Most food stylists have experience working in advertising, book or magazine publishing.

Training: Many food stylists apprentice under a more senior food stylist. Some learn the tricks of the trade by assisting on photoshoots as editorial assistants or coordinators. Some food stylists are totally self-taught, forging their own way and learning through trial and error.

Restrictions: None.

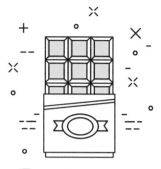

Food taster

Are you a champion eater? Have you been known to put away huge amounts of food in one sitting? Is your dedication to eating the stuff that legends are made of? Have you made it your life's mission to taste every flavour of soda on the market? If so, the glorious, wondrous life of a food taster sounds like the perfect career for you.

Most of us never think about what goes on behind the scenes before products arrive on supermarket shelves or fast food menus, but the reality is that product development is a serious business and food tasters play a very important role in it. With companies duking it out for the consumer dollar, food brands need to keep bringing new products, new flavours and new ranges to the table in order to satisfy the masses.

Tasting everything from pizza to ice cream, food tasters have to sample every single new menu item and product on the market. Most work for a particular company, so they end up tasting the same products over and over again – one food taster has been known to taste 250 types of ice cream in one day.

Working closely with the research and development team of a food brand (modern day Willy Wonkas in lab coats), food tasters test products to ensure the flavours are bang-on. Too salty? The team will remove some salt and you taste again. Too sweet? The team will remove some sugar and you taste again. Not sweet enough? Add sugar and taste again. It's this repetitive, painstaking process that ensures that only the best products end up on the consumer's table.

So who would make a good food taster? It doesn't matter if you're tasting microwave mac and cheese or flavoured oatmeal, habits like smoking can interfere with your taste buds so you need to eliminate (or minimise) smoking if you want to be a food taster. Having strong taste buds and a keen sense of smell is also important, as is having the ability to work within a team – because food tasters work with food scientists, marketers, dieticians and all sorts of other people.

This job may seem like the best thing since sliced bread, yet there are downsides to food tasting roles. Weight gain is the obvious one (some food tasters choose to spit the food out instead of swallowing, but that's considered a controversial approach among the food tasting set), but getting tired of eating all the time is another big drawback. Yes, it is possible to become fatigued from eating.

Despite the downsides to this career, it's pretty much the sweetest of deals around (unless you're a pickle taster, of course). The bottom line is you get paid to eat all day. Just try to convince people it's not the best job in the world and watch everyone break out their imaginary violins for you.

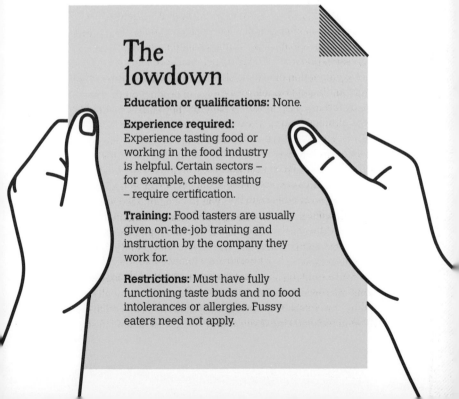

The lowdown

Education or qualifications: None.

Experience required:
Experience tasting food or working in the food industry is helpful. Certain sectors – for example, cheese tasting – require certification.

Training: Food tasters are usually given on-the-job training and instruction by the company they work for.

Restrictions: Must have fully functioning taste buds and no food intolerances or allergies. Fussy eaters need not apply.

Forensic artist

Proving that artistic ability can be used for more than just beautifying walls, forensic artists fight crime not with guns or batons but with 2B pencils and sketchpads. With their incredible ability to sketch lifelike artistic renderings of people they've never met before, forensic artists play an important part in crime reduction, sometimes without even leaving their studio.

Helping to solve crimes, forensic artists use a wide range of techniques to put together profiles of victims and people suspected of committing crimes. From using 2D and 3D imagery to recreating the likeness of an unidentified deceased person, to free-drawing the faces of criminal suspects and using data to sketch age progression portraits of missing persons, forensic artists possess a rare combination of artistic skill, technical know-how and an understanding of law enforcement.

Many forensic artists work within the police unit as a police officer, although there are exceptions to the rule. Some are retired cops who cultivate their artistic abilities after spending a life in law enforcement. A sharp understanding of criminal behaviour is needed, so many forensic artists have also studied psychology. Apart from having the required creative and technical skills, temperament plays a big part in this role. Forensic artists often have to work on challenging, confronting cases so being able to deal with the unpleasant side of this type of work is important. Viewing images of crime scenes, decomposed corpses and other disturbing things is a part of the job, so having a strong stomach and the ability to work through emotionally distressing events is crucial. Forensic artists often have to work closely with terrified victims and distraught families, so having a compassionate and understanding nature is also helpful when communicating with traumatised people.

Despite the highly serious nature of this career path, forensic art is a career well worth pursuing. With forensic artists able to influence the outcome of court cases and provide valuable tools that assist in everything from the capture of serial killers to the recovery of kidnapped children, this is a creative career that can really make an immediate difference to the world.

Some artists aspire to have their work hung in galleries, others hope to sell their work for millions, and others use their artistic skills to apprehend criminals, solve cold cases and bring closure to victims of violent crime. Forensic artists may not have their work displayed in the Guggenheim or be subject to furious bids at auction houses, but they can sleep at night knowing that their career is of the utmost value and importance to the community. Imagine the satisfaction of knowing that your composite sketch led to the arrest of a notorious murderer? Sure, you'll never be as famous as Renoir but how many lives did he save in his time at the easel?

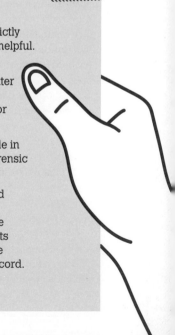

The lowdown

Education or qualifications: While not strictly necessary, a degree in fine arts would be helpful.

Experience required: Experience in graphic design, drawing and using computer programs that create facial composites is essential. Experience in law enforcement or criminal psychology is highly valued.

Training: Forensic art courses are available in many countries. Most countries require forensic artists to be certified before practising.

Restrictions: Because forensic artists need extensive knowledge of policing, law and criminal profiling, many work as part of the police force. Therefore, many forensic artists have worked (or currently work) within the police force, and do not have a criminal record.

Fortune cookie writer

Do you secretly look forward to that magical moment at the end of a Chinese meal when the fortune cookies are placed on the Lazy Susan and distributed around the table with one simple spin? Then perhaps a stint writing for fortune cookie manufacturers is in your future.

With an estimated three billion fortune cookies made and eaten each year, fortune cookie makers have a constant demand for new fortunes to be written, to avoid overuse. Of course, thousands of fortunes are rotated throughout the year to churn out a variety of these tiny pieces of paper containing everything from love advice to predictions of financial windfalls.

Yet new fortunes must always be brought to the table, in order to satisfy the masses of people who partake in regular fortune cookie eating (guilty as charged). Sure, some no doubt discard the words of wisdom after nothing more than a cursory glance, while some people take their fortunes very seriously and end up keeping their printed fortune in their purse or taping it to their work cubicle wall as a motivational tool. When you consider that a whole segment of the population carries their fortune around with them for years, fortune cookie writing becomes a bit of a high-stakes game.

Typically low-paid work aimed at graduates and aspiring writers, fortune cookie writing can generally be done from anywhere in the world, so it's the perfect job for people keen to avoid being locked into the nine-to-five grind. When you're a freelance fortune cookie writer, you can work from your bedroom at midnight, at an airport bar while waiting for a flight, or from a hammock on a tropical island. Anywhere there's an internet connection will do.

The fortune cookie has been in existence for about a century, which means coming up with original, inventive, inoffensive fortunes en masse – a tough prospect for a writer. Being charged with writing thousands of original fortunes each year, a writer needs to stay at the top of their game to keep coming up with fresh fortunes. Yes, fortune cookie-writing burnout is a thing!

Despite the pitfalls of low pay and the mental demands of having to come up with the goods over and over again, fortune cookie writing represents a unique opportunity to bust into the world of writing. With flexible work conditions and the ability to reach millions of people with your creativity, fortune cookie writing could be a fine way to hone your skills and a gateway to other writing roles – in fact, some fortune cookie writers have gone on to be published authors.

If you're a fortune cookie connoisseur and you love writing, this could be a great job for you. You may even crack open a fortune cookie after a chow mein binge at your local Chinese restaurant and find one of your own fortunes inside!

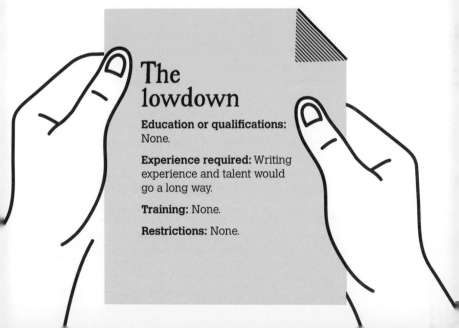

The lowdown

Education or qualifications: None.

Experience required: Writing experience and talent would go a long way.

Training: None.

Restrictions: None.

Futurist

The profession of futurism is one of those careers that will raise eyebrows. If you go down this path, some people will think you're a genius and others will think you're a seer, but then again some people will think you are totally full of it. Then there's the whole segment of the population that *still* won't understand what you do for a living despite you explaining it multiple times. With this career, you'll just have to accept that your Great Aunty Joy probably won't ever get it.

Employed by businesses and organisations to predict future technology, employment, design and social trends, futurists are able to influence everything from how buildings are designed to what technology is bought and used in an office. Futurists even influence what jobs exist within a company (no prizes for guessing that they believe there's always room for the employment of a futurist in the mix).

Although the job title sounds incredibly exciting, futurists are ordinary people who are simply very good at conducting research. Whether in the form of reading voraciously, asking professionals the right questions or studying at university, being a futurist is like being an expert in your field, except your field is evolving at such a rapid rate that it technically doesn't exist yet.

Much of the role of a futurist is related to technology. Futurists focus on what forms of tech might exist in the future and how people and organisations might use that tech. While a career in futurism would have been scoffed at decades ago, the digital age has brought an explosion of opportunities that has changed the way we work, live and relate to others. The internet, AI, social media, virtual currency, cloud computing and more have transformed our lives (I'll let you decide if that's for better or worse). Many people and companies have been left all at sea as they try to navigate through the world when there's so much choice and constant transition. This is where futurists step in.

Many professional futurists tend to work as freelancers, consulting to companies looking to safeguard the direction of their organisation. Many futurists also make a tidy profit from appearing at events, speaking at conferences and writing instructional books (which they sell at aforementioned conferences and speaking gigs). Hired by big business, government and not-for-profits to talk at meetings, conferences and workshops, futurists generally have to possess the gift of the gab in order to succeed. There is no point investing time in studying trends then hiding away in a cave and not promoting your work. That is why people who call themselves professional futurists tend to have the confidence and know-how to pull off a career that officially requires no education, qualifications or technical skills.

Essentially, a career as a futurist is a pretty smart move. Successful futurists can command six-figure salaries (without having to go to college), work on their own terms with companies of their choosing, and take their career in whatever direction they want. All that is needed is supreme confidence in yourself, an ability to network, the capacity to deliver valuable insights and the chutzpah to call yourself a futurist!

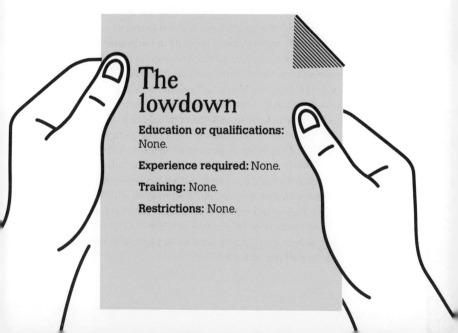

The lowdown

Education or qualifications: None.

Experience required: None.

Training: None.

Restrictions: None.

Gamer

Now here's a career that will blow the mind of your grandparents. While you may have to justify your decision (good luck having that conversation with your folks), many people have reaped considerable financial and personal rewards from embarking on a career as a pro gamer. If you regularly slay your friends in gaming marathons, this could be the career of your dreams.

Once seen as a frivolous pastime for children, or a destructive force responsible for the corruption of teens, video games are no longer considered a waste of time but a legitimate source of entertainment for adults. Thanks partly to technological developments, this billion-dollar industry now creates games that boast narratives and special effects as sophisticated as some Hollywood films.

As such, the world of eSports has exploded in recent years, with pro gamers from all walks of life competing at tournaments all over the world. From *DotA* (*Defense of the Ancients*) to *Call of Duty* and beyond, male and female gamers compete as individuals or in teams. But pro gaming championships aren't just for the elite few who have mastered the game – they also draw huge crowds of viewers, sometimes being broadcast to millions of people around the planet.

So what does it take to become a professional gamer? Thousands upon thousands of hours spent playing games is just the start. If you want to make it as a pro gamer, then you need to invest many years living and breathing the game you want to specialise in – most pro gamers choose a game and tend to stick with it. Apart from knowing the ins and outs of a particular game, pro gamers need endurance to be able to compete at a high level. Just like a professional athlete, pro gamers need to be physically and mentally fit to be able to perform at their best.

So how do pro gamers make money? And just how much can you make in a year? Most pro gamers make the bulk of their earnings by competing in championships, where prize money often totals in the millions. Many also make money from sponsorships and corporate endorsements. Although some manage to land million-dollar paydays, this isn't the case for most pro gamers. Just like other lucrative professional sports, such as tennis or golf, there are only a few at the top earning millions, and many others struggle to make ends meet until they master their craft.

Earning money from playing your favourite game sounds like the ultimate job, but the life of a professional gamer isn't all roses. Working in a high-pressure environment has its pitfalls. Hand and elbow injuries are common, fans can turn nasty when you underperform, and infighting between team members can get ugly in a pressure cooker environment like a championship.

If you choose to pursue this career path, expect many sleepless nights and much scorn from people who don't understand your choice. But your rewards could also be plenty. You could end up earning millions. You could get to travel the world to compete in tournaments. Regardless of how far you take it, as a pro gamer you get to spend your days gaming while other schmucks shuffle papers in an office. And that, my friend, is worth celebrating.

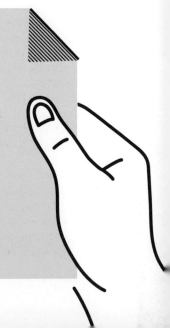

The lowdown

Education or qualifications: None.

Experience required: Thousands of hours spent gaming.

Training: None.

Restrictions: None.

Glassblower

Want to get involved in a centuries-old art form that never fails to astound people? Glassblowing is the mesmerising art of shaping molten glass by blowing and turning it to form a shape. It may not be something you've ever considered before, but if you've got a bit of artistic flair, a steady hand and a love of handmade items, then glassblowing might be a career worth investigating.

Glassblowing dates back to the Roman Empire and it's incredible to think that people are still crafting glass objects by hand. Sure, you can buy glass items that are manufactured in factories, but where's the fun in that? Items blown by hand usually have a higher value and are mainly (but not always) created for decorative purposes.

As a seriously delicate art form, only certain types of people are suited to glassblowing. Apart from being patient, glassblowers must be able to follow processes – things can get dangerous around molten glass – and have a good handle on safety procedures – get those goggles on before you start blowing. Having the artistic talent and inspiration to shape glass into works of art is also required, as the world of glass art values innovation, and buyers of glass art only want the best (and are prepared to pay for it).

Turning molten glass into objects like vases, plates and light globes, glassblowers sell their work in studios, markets, designer stores and galleries all over the world. Like many other artists, the struggle to make money is all too real, but business-savvy glassblowers have been able to turn a good profit by turning to social media to share their talents far and wide. These days, it's just not good enough to sit near the fire and wait for customers to come by – artists like glassblowers need to market themselves using a variety of methods. Contacting galleries and design stores to stock your work, sharing images of new pieces on Instagram, advising the media about your trade and business, contacting interior decorators to let them know about your pieces – all this is required if glassblowers want to earn a living from their craft.

Making a living out of a rare trade is hard work these days, so why do it? Well, continuing a craft that is practically ancient has its allure, as does working on your own business. Using your hands and breath to shape a piece of art is satisfying, as is being paid for something beautiful that you made. Glassblowers are miracle workers, magicians, alchemists, makers and more. Monetisation of this craft is tough but, if you work at it, build connections in the industry and make a name for yourself, your work could end up anywhere from galleries in London to the Guggenheim.

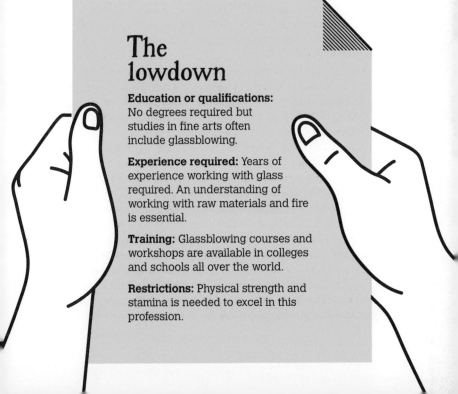

The lowdown

Education or qualifications: No degrees required but studies in fine arts often include glassblowing.

Experience required: Years of experience working with glass required. An understanding of working with raw materials and fire is essential.

Training: Glassblowing courses and workshops are available in colleges and schools all over the world.

Restrictions: Physical strength and stamina is needed to excel in this profession.

Globe maker

The perfect job for patient craftspeople who want to make their mark on the world, globe making offers the opportunity to enjoy the meditative benefits of working with your hands while creating a one-of-a-kind object that people are willing to pay thousands for.

Fashioning beautiful, detailed models of the world entirely by hand, this painstaking craft is both a rare trade and a dying art. Despite this, globe makers still exist and it could even be said that there's been a bit of a resurgence in the desire for handmade globes.

With globes taking weeks, sometimes even months, to make, globe making can't be rushed. Sure, there are mass-produced, plastic globes available for sale in stores all over the world, but a handcrafted globe made in the traditional way from plaster, metal and mahogany requires an immense amount of care and skill. Sadly, that care and skill isn't taught in any commercial courses or trade schools around the world, so the opportunity to learn can only come from taking up apprenticeships with globe makers or teaching yourself via the old, painful, trial-and-error method.

So is there any money in globe making? Well, as keenly sought items, globes made by hand are priced very highly – some globes go for hundreds of thousands of dollars. Using the best materials, and investing countless hours in perfecting the globe, globe makers can turn a profitable business but it's not without its stresses. Some globe makers offer a bespoke service where they custom-make globes for individuals in whatever colour, size and style they like. Other globe makers make a range of globes that they then either sell directly to the public or stock in high-end furniture and interiors stores. Either way, demand may be great one month and low another, so it's a fickle trade to be involved in. With most customers accustomed to getting everything they want immediately, it can be difficult to convince them to wait for weeks or months to get their product.

While not a mainstream business, globe making gives you the opportunity to keep an old tradition alive in modern times. Knowing that the items you make are treasured by the people who buy them would surely make all the hours of work that go into making a globe worthwhile. Selling a globe for a couple of hundred thousand would be a pretty sweet feeling too.

The type of role suited to perfectionists with a passion for quality craftsmanship, globe making may not be a typical path to follow, but its rewards are plenty and its influence far-reaching. To think that a handcrafted globe of yours could end up in the office of a prime minister, the study of a famous author, or the bedroom of a celebrity with an obsession for cartography – the world of globe making doesn't seem so small after all.

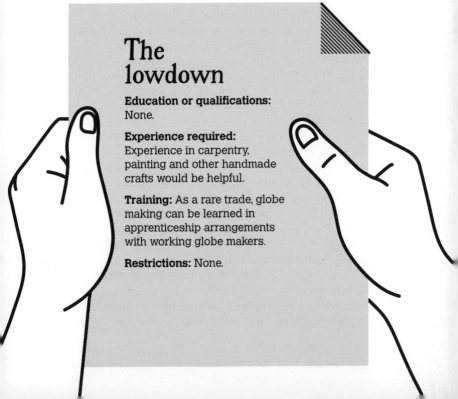

The lowdown

Education or qualifications: None.

Experience required: Experience in carpentry, painting and other handmade crafts would be helpful.

Training: As a rare trade, globe making can be learned in apprenticeship arrangements with working globe makers.

Restrictions: None.

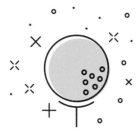

Golf ball diver

Ever played a round of golf and wondered what happened to that golf ball you just drove straight into the lake? Well, with an estimated 300 million golf balls ending up in the water in American golf courses alone, golf ball divers are onto a good thing. Golf ball divers search the water traps for the little white treasures they then clean and sell – a great way to take their diving certification and skill for treasure hunting and turn it into serious amounts of cash.

So you love diving? Sure, you could become a dive leader and take groups around coral reefs and shipwrecks. Or you could become a dive teacher and teach newbies how to dive in resort pools in tropical places. Or ... you could get into the world of golf ball retrieval and spend your days diving into murky water traps to retrieve all of those balls that didn't quite make it into the hole.

Working at courses all over the world, golf ball divers reap the rewards of doing the dirty work. Apart from having all the necessary dive certifications and correct gear, golf ball divers need a few more specific skills before being let loose in a golf course water trap. Being able to dive in the dark is necessary, as the water in the ponds and water traps at golf courses isn't exactly clear (and many golf courses insist golf ball retrieval happens after hours). Having the physical capability to handle a big, heavy bag full of golf balls is also necessary, as is the ability to do the work without damaging the green.

With most golf ball divers being independent contractors, this is a career that offers the freedom and flexibility to work whenever and wherever you want. You also get to work alone in the outdoors, which is a real bonus if you have an aversion to the following things: office politics, fluorescent light, mind-numbingly long meetings, water cooler conversations, passive aggressive post-it notes about unclean kitchens, 'team building' days, and Friday night drinks with people you secretly hate.

But this job isn't a breeze. There are serious hazards with golf ball divers encountering everything from alligators to snapping turtles. Low water temperatures are also a concern, but nothing that a good wetsuit can't counteract. But alligators? Turtles that bite? Huh? Why would anyone do this? Well, this is quite a lucrative industry with good divers able to make six-figure amounts in one year of diving.

Once they've set up the operation and have all the equipment needed to dive, transport, store and clean the balls for resale, golf ball divers also need the connections to market and sell the balls. Good operators have this all down pat and they are the ones that make the biggest amounts of cash. Sure, it's a bit of a strange business to get involved in, but if you're unafraid of water, the dark, alligators, turtles and the prospect of drowning, then golf ball diving could be a fast track to a six-figure salary without having to study or climb the corporate ladder. Now that's a real hole in one.

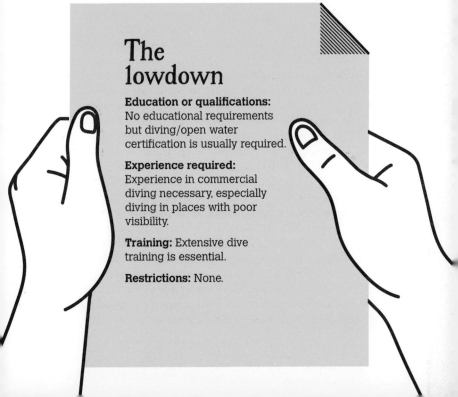

The lowdown

Education or qualifications:
No educational requirements but diving/open water certification is usually required.

Experience required:
Experience in commercial diving necessary, especially diving in places with poor visibility.

Training: Extensive dive training is essential.

Restrictions: None.

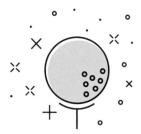

Golf course designer

If you're a bit of a golf nut and have a knack for architecture and design, why not combine the two and have the definitive career for golf freaks with architecture skills? Sure, you could easily spend your days designing things like residential homes and office blocks, then indulge your passion for golf on the weekends. But you could also pursue a career as a golf course designer and live the absolute dream.

Just as architects and landscape designers work on planning and building things like homes, offices, public parks, hotels, hospitals and government buildings, there are other spaces that also need to be designed and built, and golf courses are no exception.

Found in residential complexes, holiday resorts, tropical islands and country estates, golf courses range from straightforward to complex. Depending on the budget, allocated space, environmental factors and key target market, golf courses incorporate lakes, hills, greens, scrub, trees, fairways, footpaths, sand bunkers and more. Many properties often also incorporate buildings such as clubhouses, bars, restaurants and parking garages for golf buggies.

Apart from being accessible, visually appealing and environmentally sound, golf courses need to be built with the user's needs in mind, and this is where the creativity really comes into it. With more than half a million golf holes scattered across the globe – you can find golf courses everywhere from Barbados to Bristol – it's important to design a course with a point of difference. Golf courses need to be interesting enough to hold a golfer's attention and challenging enough to give them a reason to return, yet not so challenging that their spirit (and swing) is broken.

The technical proficiency to be a golf course designer is essential: the ability to draft plans, utilise relevant software, and understand the materials used in building, urban planning and property development. The ability to communicate and mediate with all parties – clients, government agencies, environmental groups, builders, engineers – is important, so is having an analytical, problem-solving mind. Having a solid understanding of the game of golf is paramount as there's no point planning a beautiful, innovative course that no golfer would want to play on.

Golf course design is very competitive, but it's entirely possible to build a career in this line of work. Your best bet would be to operate in countries or areas known to have a strong golf culture and plenty of golf courses. Scotland, Ireland, Australia, New Zealand, the USA, Canada, Sweden, Japan, France, Germany and South Korea all have a high number of golf courses.

If you work hard at this, you could end up designing an award-winning course favoured by the greats of the golf world! Golf claps all round for that.

The lowdown

Education or qualifications: A degree in architecture or landscape design is essential.

Experience required: Apart from having architecture or landscape design experience, golf course designers must have an inherent understanding of the game. Because of this, many golf course designers have previously worked in areas relating to professional golf.

Training: Most golf course designers cut their teeth completing internships with design firms while studying architecture or landscape design. They initially work on small-scale projects and, after learning on the job, they typically progress to designing large courses or owning their own firm.

Restrictions: None.

Greeting card writer

Do you want your writing to be read by millions of people all over the world? Many writers struggle to find an audience for their work, but the writers employed to craft the greetings inside Hallmark cards are guaranteed that their work will reach a large and varied audience.

Popularised by the character played by Joseph Gordon-Levitt in *(500) Days of Summer*, it's clear there's no glory or fame attached to being a professional greeting card writer, but there are many other benefits that make this creative career an enticing one. Firstly, you get paid a wage to write – something that represents the Holy Grail for many an unemployed or underemployed writer. Secondly, your work is shared with a very wide audience – much wider than the circulation of most print newspapers or the number of clicks an average online article receives. So with greeting card writing you get a steady income and a huge readership. The dream for most writers, right?

Usually working in an office, greeting card writers work year-round, creating clever copy for cards of all kinds that celebrate and commemorate everything from weddings to engagements, anniversaries, graduations and birthdays. The writers are charged with developing text about a wide range of topics.

With the art of creating mass-produced greeting cards being an exercise in pure sentimentality, cynics, grumps and grinches need not apply for this role. Perfectly suited for talented writers with an optimistic streak and an inventive approach to their craft, greeting card writing represents an opportunity to bring joy and comfort to the lives of people you'll never meet.

The ability to write to a brief is also a fundamental skill needed to be a successful greeting card writer. There is no point coming up with a witty zinger if your assignment is to write copy for a condolence card. Setting aside your burning feelings of contempt for Valentine's Day is a necessary skill, so is burying your atheist leanings when it comes to Easter and Christmas time. When you're a greeting card writer, you need to deliver the goods time and time again, regardless of the occasion, irrespective of how you're feeling. Think of yourself as a vessel for sprinkling sunshine all over the world and you'll go far.

So with the digital age transforming the way we communicate, is there a long-term future in greeting card writing? Admittedly, the market share of large greeting card companies is in decline. However, 6.5 billion greeting cards are still purchased in the USA every year. And in the UK, greeting card sales are up year-on-year. So, while digital communication is changing the industry, greeting cards still have a place in society. If you want to be really savvy about this creative career, look to the emerging trends. Unique, quirky greetings cards are on the up, as are progressive greeting cards that use inclusive language and imagery (think LGBTQI + wedding). Greeting card companies that remain nimble and responsive to global trends will weather the digital storm. If you're thinking of becoming a greeting card writer, hitch your creative wagon to a progressive star and you'll all but guarantee career longevity.

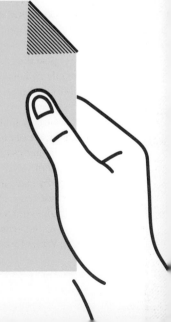

The lowdown

Education or qualifications: None, but a degree in Arts, Media or Communications would be helpful.

Experience required: Writing experience is usually necessary to be hired as a greeting card writer.

Training: None.

Restrictions: None.

Heli-ski guide

This is a dream job for anyone allergic to working indoors and the worst nightmare for anyone afraid of heights, cold weather or physical exertion. Heli-ski guides work with ski operators, remote lodges and luxury ski resorts to lead experienced skiers to some of the world's most challenging ski runs.

If you're a seasoned snow bunny, sure you could spend your days teaching children to snowplough their way down mini-slopes or helping beginners to master the art of getting onto a T-bar lift without getting dragged head first through the powder. Or you could pull the ultimate badass ski career manoeuvre and train to become a heli-ski guide.

Working everywhere from Canada to the USA, Japan and Chile, heli-ski guides are an elite branch of ski instructors who possess a range of skills above and beyond what is required of a typical ski guide. Leading groups of people on multi-day ski trips from remote lodges and day skiing stints from mountains and glaciers, heli-ski guides specialise in safely skiing in extremely remote locations only accessible by helicopter.

Supreme skiing and snowboarding talent is essential to becoming a heli-ski guide, because if you can't handle a black run with ease then you're not skilled enough to train others or keep them safe. When it comes to heli-skiing, hands-on experience is everything, so heli-ski guides have hundreds, if not thousands of skiing hours behind them.

Other key skills and training you must have include: first aid certifications, the ability to detect avalanche risks, knowledge of snow rescue and helicopter safety procedures, an understanding of weather patterns, and a talent for delivering topnotch customer service. While this is a risky profession, it's all about taking *calculated* risks – not blindly leaping off cliffs. As such, heli-ski instructors usually need to go through specific training and certification in order to gain work.

It's not a career for the faint hearted and there are plenty of rewards that come with being the job. Spending most of their time working in the great outdoors, heli-ski instructors get to work in some of the world's most jaw-dropping locations. With no day being the same, there is plenty of variety in this role as there's always new terrain to ski, new guests to meet and new weather conditions creating complex problems to solve with creativity and ingenuity.

On the bad days, you might lose feeling in your fingers, take a painful tumble in a blizzard or have to deal with a guest freaking out about going in a helicopter for the first time, but even your worst days will be better spent than sitting in a mind-numbingly long, unproductive office meeting listening to people use words like 'pivot', 'innovation' and 'growth mindset'.

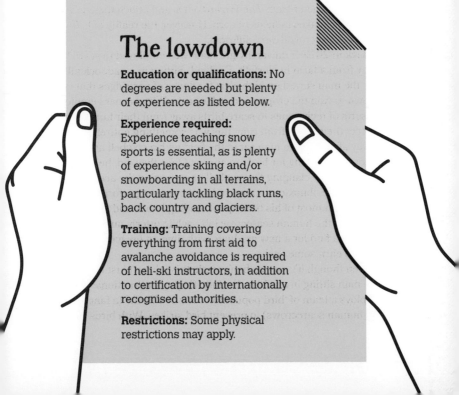

The lowdown

Education or qualifications: No degrees are needed but plenty of experience as listed below.

Experience required: Experience teaching snow sports is essential, as is plenty of experience skiing and/or snowboarding in all terrains, particularly tackling black runs, back country and glaciers.

Training: Training covering everything from first aid to avalanche avoidance is required of heli-ski instructors, in addition to certification by internationally recognised authorities.

Restrictions: Some physical restrictions may apply.

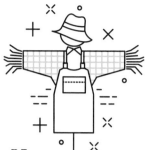

Human scarecrow

Human whaaaaat? I know your brain is full of questions about this one. No, I'm not making this up – a few people in the world have been employed as scarecrows. Sure, this is a bit of a gag job that very few people in the world actually follow as a career, but it's too good an example of the extremely bizarre ways in which people can earn money to not include here. Keep reading if you're even a little bit curious about what a human scarecrow does.

You'd be forgiven for thinking that human scarecrows dress up like the character from *The Wizard of Oz* and attach themselves to wooden stakes in fields of corn. However, the reality of being a human scarecrow is very different.

Back in 2012, a university graduate was employed to scare birds away from a farm in Norfolk, England. Sitting in a paddock all day, the man stayed on high alert for flocks of partridges that were known to ruin the crop on a regular basis. With farmers employing all sorts of techniques to scare birds away from their farms and protect their crops from ruin, this was something entirely new.

Day after day, the man sat in the field with a cowbell and an accordion, waiting for birds to appear. Once they did, he chased them away by clanging the cowbell or squeezing the accordion to make the obnoxious sound so loved by street performers in Paris. With most of his time spent reading books and listening to podcasts, the human scarecrow job – while utterly nuts – proved to be quite a find for a new graduate with time on his hands and the need to earn some cash.

Even though it's rare as hen's teeth, this job isn't just limited to one man sitting in a field in Norfolk. Beijing International Airport employs a team of 'bird population control officers' (a fancy way to say human scarecrows) to prevent bird strikes. With birds flying into aircraft engines representing a significant safety threat and cost to airlines, this is actually a very serious role.

Oh yes, Beijing International Airport has a bird problem of Hitchcockian proportions. Flocks of swallows regularly congregate on the runways, and the airport has even been shut down on several occasions, causing all sorts of havoc and financial losses for passengers and airlines. In response to this, the team of human scarecrows work around the clock to prevent birds from entering the airspace. Using a range of devices and tactics – coloured flags, wire mesh, automatic gas exploders, bird distress recorders – this is a military-style operation on a truly epic scale. The human scarecrows even spray pesticides on surrounding grassed areas to remove bugs commonly eaten by birds.

Although it's a serious business, no education requirements are needed to fulfil these types of roles. Just a willingness to do whatever it takes to get flocks of birds the hell away from whatever property you're protecting. Vigilance is required, as is the ability to think up creative ways to annoy birds. Human scarecrow work might not win you any awards or reap huge financial benefits, but you'll have a kooky little career that almost no one else in the world has (and a very cool answer to write in the 'profession' box on legal documents).

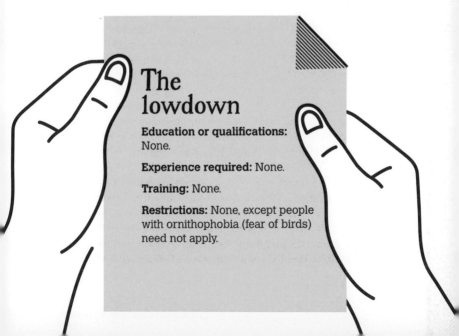

The lowdown

Education or qualifications: None.

Experience required: None.

Training: None.

Restrictions: None, except people with ornithophobia (fear of birds) need not apply.

Instagrammer

For most of us, Instagram is a place where we upload images of our pets doing cute things and photos of beach trips that look great after a few filters have been applied. Then there are the anointed ones who have turned the fine art of Instagramming into a career.

All around the world there are people getting paid to Instagram – and some are earning seriously big bucks. One of the largest groups of professional Instagrammers are the travel Instagrammers. These people travel the world on someone else's dime, often receiving free flights, accommodation and experiences in exchange for a series of posts highlighting the destination. Professional Instagrammers who specialise in taking travel shots typically also charge a fee per post or per trip. With some of them being paid thousands of dollars per day, Instagramming can be quite lucrative.

So, who is paying them to trounce around the world snapping sunsets as they go? Tourism bodies, hotel chains and airlines are the biggest users of professional Instagrammers, while Instagrammers who focus on the lifestyle market are paid by clothing labels and beauty brands. This relatively new way for brands to engage with consumers means that Instagrammers are often required to disclose to their audience when they are paid for posts.

I know you're asking, 'Just how easy is it to rise through the ranks and end up at the top as a paid Instagrammer?'. Well, it's not as easy as adding #wanderlust to all your posts. You'll need to be really handy with a camera and you'll also need to be able to spend plenty of time cultivating a following. Obviously the more followers and interactions you have on your account, the higher the fee you can command. You'll need to go to great lengths to get the 'money shot' that will attract thousands of likes, so that means getting up early to snap sunrises from tops of mountains and spending hours waiting around with your camera for whales to breach. And forget ever eating a meal without styling and photographing it first.

While this may sound like the ultimate dream job, there are definitely downsides. If you're always travelling the world, then you've almost always got jet lag and are missing your friends and family back home. As a platform that trades on immediacy and demands near-constant interaction, professional Instagrammers are often slaves to their tech. Forced to constantly upload, comment, like and respond to their followers in an effort to retain them, to bring in new followers and increase engagement, the life of a professional Instagrammer is a carousel that never stops. The platform is a hungry beast that constantly needs to be fed with new content, so you'll have to keep finding new sunsets, cresting waves and brunch spreads to snap.

On the upside, you'll get paid to travel the world and you can work from anywhere with an internet connection. You'll receive loads of free stuff, get to have many cool experiences and meet lots of people. It's a mighty sweet gig as long as you don't mind being married to your smartphone.

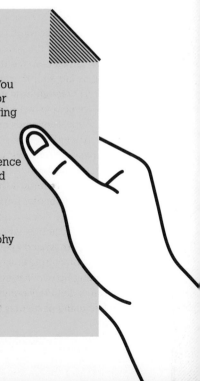

The lowdown

Education or qualifications: No formal education requirements. You could be a high school dropout or have a PhD – the intellectual playing field is level on the Instagram platform.

Experience required: No experience required to set up an account and start your journey.

Training: While there's no formal training involved, a high-quality camera and advanced photography skills are helpful.

Restrictions: None. If you have a smartphone and an Instagram account, then you're in the game.

Laughter therapist

Has anyone ever accused you of having a laugh? If so, set yourself up as a laughter therapist and you might just end up laughing yourself all the way to the bank.

In case you missed the memo, life isn't a barrel of laughs for many people. With illness, unemployment, financial difficulties, relationship troubles, family conflict, global meltdowns and a litany of life's annoyances creating all sorts of emotional problems, it's all too easy to take out our stress on others.

Stress management is a huge buzzword in wellness circles and, while there are a number of ways to manage stress – yoga, meditation, medication, exercise, sleep, smashing things – laughter therapy is one of the strangest, but also perhaps one of the most effective. If you have a gift for making others laugh, then keep reading as laughter therapy could be for you.

Delivering laughter workshops, seminars and programs to all sorts of people including school children, dementia patients, corporate professionals and community groups, laughter therapists use the power of laughter to help people to reduce their stress levels, bond with others, cultivate positivity and improve their outlook on life.

With multiple studies showing that laughter reduces stress hormones and boosts immunity levels, laughter therapy isn't just some feel-good lark favoured by the crystal-wearing woo-woo set. Oh no – laughter therapy can actually have immediate positive impacts on people, but what do people get from laughter therapy that they can't get from sitting down to watch a box set of *Seinfeld* episodes?

Cracking up watching your favourite sit-com on the couch by yourself is definitely beneficial, but laughter therapists facilitate laughter using particular techniques that go far beyond slapstick comedy. If working with a corporate group, laughter will be used to facilitate stronger bonds between the team so they can defuse tough situations within the workplace and work in tandem with greater ease. In a hospital setting, group laughter therapy is often deployed as a way to get vulnerable people to open up, while also adding some lightness to somewhat sad situations.

Part yoga, part meditation, part spoken word performance, laughter therapy is the type of career suited to people with backgrounds in counselling, performance, teaching and psychology. You don't need a particular degree to become a laughter therapist (because you're not an actual therapist), but there are training courses and certifications you can attain to start teaching laughter therapy to others.

As far as careers go, this one may not make you famous or deliver millions into your bank account, but you'll be surrounded by laughter each and every working day, and that is most definitely a win when considering how drab so many workplaces are. Turns out, laughter isn't just the best medicine; it's also the best career for some.

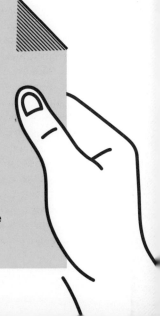

The lowdown

Education or qualifications: No degree required.

Experience required: Experience working with vulnerable people in educational or hospital settings is beneficial. Experience presenting in front of groups is helpful, with experience in performance, counselling, teaching or psychology also useful.

Training: Laughter therapy certification is available via a short training course.

Restrictions: Criminal record checks might be required, especially if working with children.

Letterpress printer

Are you a bit of a stationery aficionado? Do you fawn over beautifully embossed, foil-edged wedding invites? Do you have drawers filled with beautiful, bespoke note paper you love too much to use? Then dedicating your life to letterpress printing could be a sound career choice for you.

Using a large printing press, letterpress printing is a technique that dates back to the 15th century. Before the arrival of computers and the much cheaper and faster offset printing method, all books and other printed materials were created by hand on the letterpress using embossed letters and ink. Going the way of the dodo in the eighties and nineties, letterpress printing has enjoyed a bit of a revival of late thanks to a small band of dedicated artisans. From Melbourne to Berlin, Brooklyn, Edinburgh and Auckland, letterpress studios have popped up in many of the world's major cities.

But in the days of e-cards, digital printers and Facebook invitations, why is letterpress printing still a thing? Despite being a more costly and time-consuming form of printing, many letterpress businesses are doing quite well. While a certain portion of the population want fast, cheap ways to communicate, there's another that values small businesses, supports the resurrection of rare trades and most of all, loves looking at and creating beautiful things. And there's no doubt about it, a handcrafted and printed letterpress invitation is a mini work of art, far superior to those created in a mass print run (and let's not even compare it to a Facebook invitation because they're not even in the same stratosphere).

Enterprising letterpress printers can make money in numerous ways. They can offer design and printing services to clients who want custom wedding invitations, signage for corporate events or bespoke materials to support marketing campaigns. They can create their own range of unique greeting cards and art to sell in stores. They can also teach others the art of letterpress printing and make money from running courses and workshops.

The perfect career choice for any nostalgic soul with a love of stationery, typography and calligraphy, the life of a letterpress printer is infused with creativity every step of the way. From mixing inks to create the ideal colour, to designing invitations and selecting paper stock, letterpress printing is an art form that requires patience, dedication and a way with words.

Considered a rare trade, letterpress printing is a skill typically learned as an apprentice. Apprenticeships are quite rare, and many letterpress printers start out by simply buying an antique press and learning the process through a combination of trial and error. Apart from having the technical know-how needed to run a press, letterpress printers should also possess good customer service skills, a knack for design and a good understanding of the stationery market. On top of that, letterpress studio owners also require all the marketing, administration and management skills needed to run a successful business.

If all that sounds fine and dandy, the lovely letterpress life could be for you.

The lowdown

Education or qualifications: None.

Experience required: Experience operating a letterpress helps, although it's a skill that can be taught.

Training: Most letterpress printers learn the trade as part of an apprenticeship. Some letterpress printers also offer courses for those wishing to be trained in the art.

Restrictions: None.

Life drawing model

Are you comfortable with getting your kit off in front of strangers? Do you have a deep fascination for the greats of the art world? Do you like the idea of being immortalised in art? Then embarking on a career as a life drawing model sounds like a good idea.

First up, let's set things straight. Life modelling is not posing for pornography or adult magazines, doing a striptease or burlesque performance or giving a pay-per-view show for fetishists. Life modelling is posing naked for artists who sketch or paint your form either for pleasure, study or profit. As a profession it's existed for centuries. Think of all the nude men and women hanging in public and private art galleries around the world – in all likelihood, most of them would have been paid life models.

Most people pursue this type of work on a part-time basis, but it is possible to enjoy a full-time career in life modelling if you work hard to build connections within the industry and market yourself to potential employers. Enterprising life models can find many different avenues of work if they're savvy. From modelling in small, private art schools to sitting for art students at prestigious colleges, posing for working artists and even hosting life drawing classes and parties for private groups – this is very popular for corporate team-building events, hens' nights and milestone birthdays – there are many ways to make money from being a life model. Some even teach life modelling workshops to aspiring models.

It would be tempting to think that all life models need to do is take their clothes off and stand still, but there's actually more to it than that. Knowing how to hold a pose for long periods is essential, as is being able to take direction from others – you will be asked to pose a certain way, in specific positions. Having a thick skin is important, to deal with the rare instances of snickering or laughing from your onlookers, as well as having an open mind and collaborative approach to your work – the artists don't want a lifeless, rigid person posing in front of them. Great art requires vulnerability, openness and honesty and it's the role of the life model to infuse that into their work.

Sure, if you pursue this career some people may not understand your choice (your grandparents probably won't get it) but there are plenty of rewards on offer. The best part about this career is that almost anyone on the planet could do it, if they wanted. And no, you don't have to have killer abs or cellulite-free legs to be a life model. This type of work is open to all body shapes and types, male and female, young and elderly. Actually, having an interesting body with curves, kinks, wrinkles and dimples makes for a good life model because it's much more interesting to sketch a variety of body types rather than people who look like they've been churned out of the supermodel factory.

Viewed by many as an empowering career choice for men and women, life models get to contribute to the education of young artists and work with a wide variety of people – maybe even with the greats of the art world (if they're lucky). Most of all, life models get to tell people they undress for a living – it's the ultimate dinner party icebreaker.

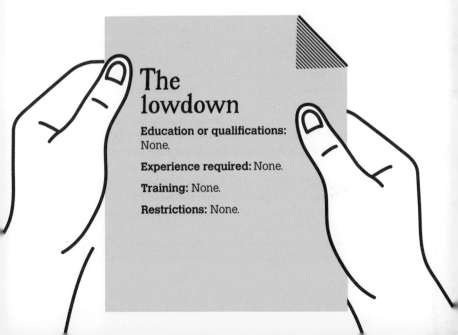

The lowdown

Education or qualifications: None.

Experience required: None.

Training: None.

Restrictions: None.

Location scout

Do you fancy getting paid to jet about, scouring the planet for the ultimate locations to shoot films, television programs and commercials? Would you like to be able to point at the television screen during an episode of *Game of Thrones* and say 'That's Iceland. You know how I know that? I flew to Iceland, then got a chopper to that exact spot, then recommended it as the place to film this scene.' While your friends may not want to watch TV or movies with you ever again, the life of a location scout involves so much travel you'll hardly be at home anyway.

As one of the more exotic, exciting jobs within the film and television sector, the road to becoming a location scout is not easy but, then again, it's not impossible either. As a position that is coveted by many, you'll be competing against a serious amount of people who want to get into the industry. Despite that, becoming a location scout doesn't require university degrees or long periods of study – any hardworking, enterprising person with a good handle on the film industry can have a crack at location scouting.

Although highly competitive, when you think about all the films, documentaries, TV series and ads that are made around the world every year, there's a fair chunk of location scouting work to be had.

Responding to very specific briefs from directors, location scouts must have a firm understanding of the script before even contemplating starting to look for the perfect location. From hunting down the ultimate trail to shoot an epic mountain-biking scene to finding a Victorian-era home that would suit a period piece, location scouts have to be patient, communicative and dogged in their pursuit for the best locations.

Taking into account an array of factors, including local weather patterns, the country's security situation, costs involved in shooting, the granting of permits to film and any number of unexpected issues, being a location scout requires much more than turning up, looking around and saying 'This'll do'.

Having an understanding of the creative processes that go into filmmaking – for example, lighting and set design – is essential, so is having excellent interpersonal skills (in order to get along with the film crew and producers, sometimes in trying circumstances). Possessing the ability to get things done no matter what, and merging creativity with logistical prowess, good location scouts are a rare breed.

What lies on the other side of the long hours, late nights, weekends and time spent in transit between countries is a remarkable career that can take you literally anywhere. From the jungles of Brazil to the souks of Morocco, the wilds of Alaska, and the gritty streets of New York, anywhere on the planet is a potential film location. Apart from the travel opportunities, location scouts get to work with influential filmmakers and actors, and help to shape movies and television series that are loved by millions. If that's not enough incentive, you may also get to meet Brad Pitt at some stage.

The lowdown

Education or qualifications: None.

Experience required: Experience working within the film and TV production industry helps.

Training: Most location scouts learn the ropes while working as assistants or researchers on film shoots and television programs, rising through the ranks as they go. Some are journalists or researchers that choose to specialise in a particular region or country, for example, South East Asia. Either way, there's no real training program for this type of job; it's a learn-as-you-go affair.

Restrictions: Must have the ability to travel widely.

Luxury property caretaker

The perfect job for someone with Champagne taste but a beer budget, becoming a luxury property caretaker is a sneaky way to get a taste of the good life without living beyond your means.

From private islands owned by billionaires to government-owned castles filled with heritage treasures, deluxe beach houses in remote locations and luxury homes on sprawling estates, these properties require caretakers to live on site to ensure it is safe, secure and well maintained when the owner is away.

With many upscale properties containing priceless art and important personal effects, live-in caretakers ensure that the property isn't left vacant and open to abuse by thieves and squatters. Also, caretakers make sure the place is liveable for when an owner decides to pop in and stay (even though that may be for only a handful of weeks in a year).

Sounds pretty good? Well, to be suitable for a role like this you'd have to be happy living in another, often isolated, location. You'd also want to be sure you're able to respect the privacy of the owner and are discreet enough to not leak personal info to the media if caretaking a home for a celebrity. Being honest and trustworthy enough to not throw a wild party at a multi-million dollar estate is also necessary. Same goes for not taking the boss's Cadillac for a spin without their permission.

Duties can vary depending on the type of property, with coordinating maintenance and repair work to light gardening being commonplace tasks. Some roles also include animal care such as feeding horses and walking dogs, as well as everyday things like dealing with mail, deliveries and visitors. Depending on the size of the property and the duties required, many roles like this go to couples who work in tandem to take care of the house and grounds.

Some property caretakers work all year round, while others only work seasonally – caretakers might need to look after a beach house in winter, then vacate throughout the summer when it's in use. Some caretakers move from short-term role to short-term role, others take it on as a full-time job, staying put in one place for years.

Payment for this type of work is usually average considering your home base and power bills are taken care of, so if you want to make millions, this is not a good idea. But if you want to be *surrounded* by millions then sure, this is a good way to live a mortgage-free lifestyle in a premier location.

With this type of work available everywhere from Barbados to the Hamptons, England, France and Cape Town, it would be wise to start doing house-sitting gigs in order to understand what's required of you. From there, signing up to caretaking websites and companies that place caretakers in residences is a good way to put yourself out there. Who knows ... depending on where you can work, you could end up in a mansion in Hawaii, a castle in Scotland or a private island owned by a successful entrepreneur. In any case, this is a job that can land you in some truly unforgettable places – all without needing a degree, connections or much experience. Sign me up!

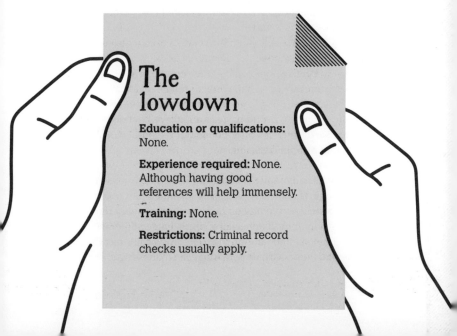

The lowdown

Education or qualifications: None.

Experience required: None. Although having good references will help immensely.

Training: None.

Restrictions: Criminal record checks usually apply.

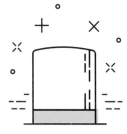

Magician

Now here's a great career for anyone with a gift for disappearing from parties without being detected or for pulling coins from behind unsuspecting people's ears. Instead of schlepping to work in a depressing office building each day, magicians use their time on this earth to make magic happen. And what a worthy pursuit that is.

In case you haven't noticed, magic has moved on from the days of sawing women in half and then putting them back together (thankfully). These days, magicians have an impressive range of stunts, illusions, miraculous escapes and other tricks that leave audiences scratching their heads wondering what they just saw.

Whether you choose to focus on being an escape artist or go the traditional 'rabbit out of a hat' route, there is a demand for magicians to perform in a number of places. Everywhere from suburban backyard birthday parties to huge arenas in Las Vegas, magicians bring wonder, excitement and a little bit of old-school razzle-dazzle to audiences all over the world.

While it looks like a fun, light career move, being a magician isn't as easy as donning a cape and pointing a wand at a top hat. Magic is a very serious business indeed. Becoming a successful, in-demand magician requires years and years of study and practice. From pulling off tricks to developing a fresh routine and cultivating a sense of showmanship, magicians work very hard to make magic happen. Some attend academies while others are self-taught, but what binds all magicians together is firm dedication to their profession. So that means practising for hours and hours, turning up to perform late at night and on the weekends, and investing a fair bit of money in things such as props, costumes and make-up.

If all this seems too daunting then it's important to recognise the rewards that come with being a magician, like being able to connect with audiences, bring joy, avoid the old nine-to-five grind and get paid for wearing over-the-top costumes. And if you hit the big time like David Copperfield, then you can also abracadabra yourself up some serious cash too.

With the majority of magicians working independently, magicians need to have next-level business skills and a gift for self-promotion. There's no point having the trick of the century if you don't know how to market it. So building connections within the industry and having the confidence to market yourself is critical. Because no matter how good a magician you are, you still can't conjure up audiences out of a hat.

In an increasingly cynical world, leading a life dedicated to the pursuit of magic is a bold move. Your parents may not approve, but at least you can throw a smoke bomb and disappear every time they voice their disapproval!

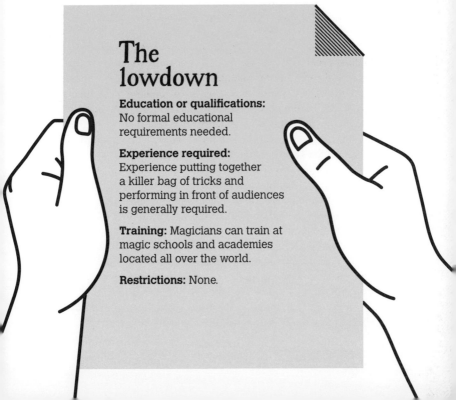

The lowdown

Education or qualifications: No formal educational requirements needed.

Experience required: Experience putting together a killer bag of tricks and performing in front of audiences is generally required.

Training: Magicians can train at magic schools and academies located all over the world.

Restrictions: None.

Master distiller

Are you partial to a tipple of whisky? Do you feel you have a refined palate? Do you love the smell of malt? Then working in a spirit distillery as a master distiller would be your ultimate career move.

Being in charge of a distillery is one of those careers that elicits a 'get outta town' response from people. However, it's entirely possible to rise to the top and take over the operations of a distillery – as long as you're prepared to dedicate many years to learning the trade, developing a palate and establishing the skills necessary to manage a timeworn, concise process that can't be fast tracked, bastardised or meddled with.

An umbrella job title used to describe anyone who oversees the distilling process at a spirit distillery – usually whisky, but it can also include other spirits such as gin – a master distiller must have a firm handle on the business, from distilling techniques to ingredients, bottling processes and marketing. In fact, many master distillers spend plenty of time performing brand ambassadorial duties by attending industry events, dinners and competitions.

Being a distiller isn't only about slowly tasting your way around barrels of spirits. It's an all-encompassing role that takes years of dedication and hard work to perfect. The hours are often long and with so many different technical and environmental elements impacting on the final product – for example, temperature, equipment, human labour, ingredient quality – it's difficult to ensure the consistent quality of each batch. Patience is needed, so is commitment to your craft. Being able to work through challenges is crucial, and having a good work ethic to ensure you're able to work around the clock is key. You'll be happy to hear that developing a palate is also incredibly important, so drinking a wide range of spirits is an integral part of this role. Tasting and retasting your own product, time and time again throughout the process is hard work, but someone's got to do it, right?

Whether you choose to pursue an interest in Kentucky bourbon or Scotch whisky, most distillers tend to stick with one type of spirit, such is the delicate, detailed nature of learning how to run a distillery. If whisky is your thing, you couldn't just walk into a gin distillery and take over the reins. Once you're into distilling, you tend to be in it for life, this is why the stereotypical master distiller is a senior gentleman who has spent decades working in a distillery.

While this is a pretty rare role, there are thousands of distilleries around the world. Distilleries can be found in both rural and urban locations in countries like Scotland, England, the USA, Australia and Japan. Some distilleries have existed on country estates for centuries, while others have popped up in inner-city warehouses.

If you choose to work in an inner-city gin distillery in Melbourne or a historic whisky distillery in Scotland, this is one career worth raising a glass to.

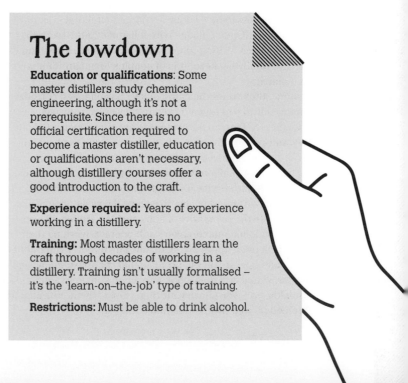

The lowdown

Education or qualifications: Some master distillers study chemical engineering, although it's not a prerequisite. Since there is no official certification required to become a master distiller, education or qualifications aren't necessary, although distillery courses offer a good introduction to the craft.

Experience required: Years of experience working in a distillery.

Training: Most master distillers learn the craft through decades of working in a distillery. Training isn't usually formalised – it's the 'learn-on-the-job' type of training.

Restrictions: Must be able to drink alcohol.

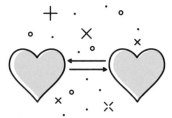

Matchmaker

Are you one of those people who always tries to set up your friends? Can't help but throw a dinner party when you have two single friends that you just *know* will be perfect together? Then the romance-infused life of a professional matchmaker might just be for you!

Your friends and family may call it meddling, but when you are a professional matchmaker running your own successful consultancy it's not called meddling, it's business. And don't forget – professional matchmakers have existed in many different cultures for centuries.

Taking many different forms depending on which culture you belong to, in times gone by a professional matchmaker might have travelled from village to village with a list of eligible bachelors and bachelorettes waiting to find their best match, assessing the genetic and family backgrounds of couples to ensure they were a suitable match.

Of course, these days the game of love has changed considerably, with many cultures taking a more liberal view of marriage, seeing it as much more than an agreement to secure property, financial stability and genetic diversity. These days, people tend to want to marry for love and this is where modern matchmakers come in.

Matchmakers usually run their own consultancy businesses, offering a boutique service for singles who are searching for 'the one' and don't mind paying to secure the assistance of an expert. Despite the popularity of apps such as Tinder, all over the world old-fashioned matchmakers still operate, working their hardest to ensure Cupid's arrow reaches its target. Professional matchmakers operate on the premise that they have many 'high quality' individuals on their books, so when you go to a professional matchmaker, you won't have your time wasted by the riffraff and bottom feeders that dwell on online dating sites.

Facilitating introductions between two 'high quality' individuals with similar interests and worldviews isn't as easy as it seems. Most matchmakers insist on all candidates filling out a lengthy questionnaire so they can get a good read on who you'd best suit, and some insist on face-to-face meetings before taking candidates on as clients (a good way to weed out liars, phonies and the delusional).

These days, many savvy matchmakers fill niches by providing their services to specific groups of people. There are professional matchmakers for seniors, millionaires and the LGBTQI community. By focusing on one subset of the population, matchmakers have been able to provide specialised services to groups of people who often find dating harder than most (although surely the Tinder for Seniors app isn't too far away).

As a profession, matchmaking is a lot like headhunting, but for a partner rather than a new career. Apart from having the good business acumen required to run your own consultancy firm, modern matchmakers need to be patient, people-friendly and empathetic. The art of matchmaking is a high-stakes game where emotions run deep, so a calm demeanour is essential, as is a degree of pragmatism (for when things inevitably don't work out between two clients).

There would be an inherent amount of job satisfaction in knowing you're bringing people together and changing the course of their lives, for better or worse.

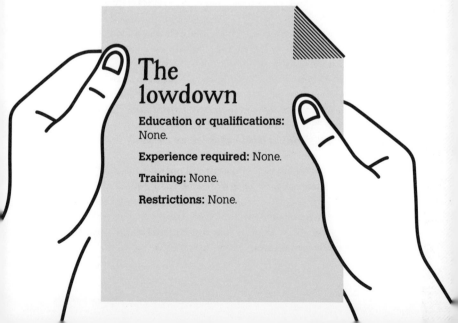

The lowdown

Education or qualifications: None.

Experience required: None.

Training: None.

Restrictions: None.

Milliner

Abraham Lincoln's stovepipe. Charlie Chaplin's bowler. Jackie Kennedy's pillbox. Indiana Jones's faded, dusty fedora. Hats have had their place in the fashion world for centuries, but how often do we think about the people that make them? Hat making, known as millinery, has been a profession for centuries. And while things have changed from the heady days of hat wearing and making, it's still a bona fide career choice for crafty types who are into fashion.

As opposed to mass-produced caps that are churned out by factories, creating handmade hats from scratch is a bit of an art form. From the elaborate, artistic creations modelled at the Kentucky Derby, Royal Ascot and Melbourne Cup each year to the sculpted modern masterpieces worn by celebrities on the red carpet and the romantic, custom-made bridal hats and veils, milliners regularly add something extra to outfits worn for special occasions.

While fewer people today are wearing hats in their everyday lives than in the 1940s, handmade hats are still popular with both men and women for special occasions, such as weddings, horse racing carnivals, and black tie dinners. Furthermore, milliners often create hats for film, television and theatre productions. Not sure there's much film work for milliners out there? Imagine watching a Winston Churchill biopic without his signature homburg, a Jane Austen film adaptation without bonnets, or Harry Potter without the Hogwarts Sorting Hat.

The art of hat making is a profession worth pursuing if you love hats, have a flair for fashion and a talent for whipping up handmade creations. You'll also need to have sewing and design skills, and a good understanding of the materials used in millinery. Most milliners learn the trade from a senior milliner or attend millinery courses at fashion institutes, although it's also possible to teach yourself the art if you already have sewing experience and the time (and patience) needed to learn through trial and error.

Apart from all the technical and artistic skills required to successfully make hats, most milliners run their own businesses, so having a good handle on marketing, networking, pricing and business administration is needed. Working one-on-one with most clients, milliners also need to have excellent customer service skills and an eye for the latest trends, as there's no point pushing pork pie hats if all the dudes in town want fedoras.

This creative career will give you the freedom and flexibility to run your own business and be involved in the dynamic world of fashion. Frequent travel to events such as fashion shows and film sets might also be on the cards. If you like the idea of spending your time making creations that could end up anywhere from the silver screen to the head of an A-List celebrity, then you might want to hang your hat on a career in millinery.

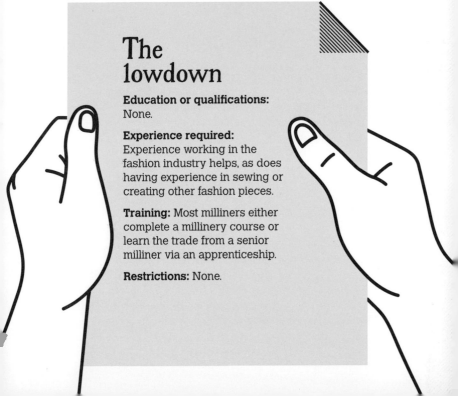

The lowdown

Education or qualifications:
None.

Experience required:
Experience working in the fashion industry helps, as does having experience in sewing or creating other fashion pieces.

Training: Most milliners either complete a millinery course or learn the trade from a senior milliner via an apprenticeship.

Restrictions: None.

Mourner

Did you miss your chance at being a Hollywood actor? Can you bung on the tears at a moment's notice? Not bothered by being in close proximity to dead bodies? Then the truly bizarre life of a professional mourner may just be your calling.

In what has to be one of the saddest indictments of how much our communities and families have been fractured by modern society, professional mourners can now be hired to fill the seats at funerals. Yep, that's right, unpopular, socially isolated (or just plain mean) people who are about to kick the bucket and know that there will be a thin crowd to send them off can just call 1800-RENT-A-MOURNER* to prearrange a solid crew of strangers to make themselves look less pathetic at their own funeral.

Presumably frustrated actors, students or just really morbid people wanting to earn a buck, professional mourners turn up to funerals and wakes in their suits, pretend to know the deceased and politely sit through the service. Some add embellishments like tears, signing the guestbook and leaning over the open casket to whisper words of love to the corpse. In cultures where mourning is expected to be a loud, expressive affair, professional mourners get into full method-acting mode, throwing themselves on the floor, wailing and crying like they've lost someone they actually knew and loved. Responsible for truly Oscar-worthy performances, those types of professional mourners deserve a higher rate of pay for their efforts.

So why on earth would someone run a professional mourning business or sign themselves up as a professional mourner? With no educational qualifications, training or special requirements for the role, this is the perfect job for someone who has no interest in studying or working in entry-level positions. It's a recession-proof industry, so that's a plus. Technically anyone can be a professional mourner, although possessing sensitivity and scrubbing up well is important (unless you're going for the dirty, estranged uncle look).

With this career, you can spin it whichever way you want. You can tell people you're an actor, or that you work in community service, or that you're a part of the funeral industry. Or you scramble their tiny little minds by being honest and telling them you're a professional mourner and you hope to work with them soon.

* Not an actual business, but might be something to think about setting up, huh?

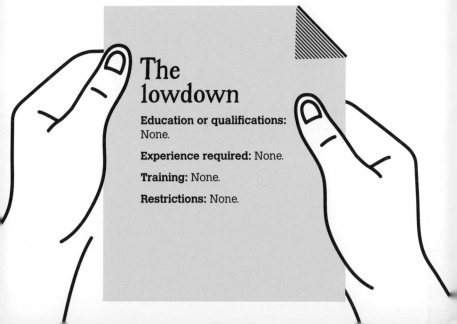

The lowdown

Education or qualifications: None.

Experience required: None.

Training: None.

Restrictions: None.

Movie body double

Body double work – a role in constant demand with film and television studios – is the perfect job for people who love the idea of working in the film industry but hate the thought of being famous. If you're hardworking, good at taking direction from others and have a body you're proud of, then body double work might be for you.

Normally used for scenes that actors don't want to do – usually scenes involving nudity, simulated sex or a difficult physical performance, for example, complicated dance moves or acrobatics – body doubles are an essential part of the film industry and the unsung heroes of many a film set. From hopping into bed with a Hollywood hunk to walking across the set with absolutely nothing on, it would be hard to find a modern, big budget movie that didn't include the work of at least one body double.

In fact, some of the most iconic film and television scenes can be attributed to body doubles. From the memorable solo dance scenes in *Flashdance* to most of the revealing scenes in *Pretty Woman* and Cersei's infamous naked walk of shame in season five of *Game of Thrones*, body doubles stand in at some of the most crucial and influential moments.

So, while body doubles have the ability to say: 'Look, there's my butt', there's little recognition for their vital work. While the big name stars who command multi-million dollar pay packets get all the glory, body doubles often receive little acclaim for their work despite millions of people seeing them on the big screen. This is a both a blessing and a curse, as body doubles can often have a fulfilling, profitable career in the movies without having the paparazzi on their doorstep or finding their outfit scrutinised on *TMZ*. Although, body doubles who actually lust for fame might want to forget body doubling and go for roles where the spotlight shines on them.

Regardless, this is a brilliant career for anyone with a love of film and a killer bod. Yes, most body doubles are required to be very slim and physically fit. Of course, there are always exceptions to the rule but, generally speaking, body doubles need to pass for famous actors, so a career in body doubling would require many hours at the gym. Then there are also the many hours spent on set waiting around for your scene to start.

Despite the lack of fame and regularly having to play the waiting game on set, this is a career unlike most, which involves travel to remote locations and regular interaction with some of film's greatest directors and actors. At the end of a successful career, most body doubles would have a body of work (pardon the pun) that most average people would kill for. They would also most likely have a body most people would kill for.

The lowdown

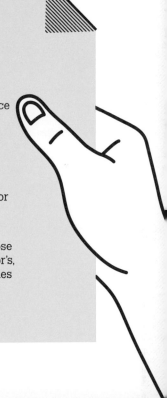

Education or qualifications: None.

Experience required: No official experience required, however, having movie credits to your name will help when building your profile. Most body doubles start in small productions, then work their way up to blockbusters.

Training: None. Although a stint in acting or film school can only help your prospects.

Restrictions: Most body doubles who do film work are very fit, slim individuals whose bodies could easily pass for a famous actor's, so body doubles need to lay off the Twinkies if they want to succeed.

National Geographic photographer

Photography jobs are among the most coveted in the world, but the undisputed peak of photography jobs is snapping your way around the world for *National Geographic*. From hanging out with Mongolian nomads to mingling with the Bedouin in Morocco, *National Geographic* photographers get to travel to some of the world's most exotic, remote and fascinating places. And the best part is, they are lucky enough to get paid for it.

One of the biggest misconceptions about photography is that it's all about mastering technical skills and equipment. Sure, you certainly need the technical skills and understanding required to take killer photos, but you also need a whole bunch of other soft skills to be a successful photographer, especially for *National Geographic*. You could study the art of photography your whole life and still not reach the calibre needed to work for *National Geographic*.

Having a firm understanding and admiration of cultures other than your own is paramount, as is having the ability to build trust with strangers, because who is going to let you take their photo if you just turn up and obnoxiously wave a camera in their face? You need to be able to work as a part of a team because most shoots involve working with assistants, fixers, porters and other crew members. Cultivating resilience and patience is also important, as photography usually involves lots of waiting around and many moments of frustration when the light isn't quite right, when someone walks through your shot, when a beautiful building you want to shoot is closed to the public, when the perfect person just won't agree to being photographed.

With travel to far-flung places being a significant part of this career, you need to be cool with all of the following: jet lag, airport queues, packing, vaccinations, diarrhoea, long bus rides on bumpy roads, lost luggage, carrying heavy loads up mountains, cross-cultural misunderstandings and being away from your friends and family for long periods of time. Dream job, huh?

One of the major factors that sets *National Geographic* photographers apart is that they are comfortable with risk and utterly obsessed with getting the shot. That's why many *National Geographic* shots are so iconic – because one obsessed photographer just wouldn't let it go. You have to be the type of person that will drown in their own sweat just to get the shot. Not every day is that brutal, but on the days it is, you need to be prepared to dig deep for your craft.

If that sounds appealing, then what on earth is wrong with you? Just kidding, if that sounds appealing then start studying the work of the masters of *National Geographic* photography, such as Steve McCurry, Joel Sartore, Lynn Johnson or David Alan Harvey. Swot up on photography techniques. Attend photography workshops. Take thousands and thousands of photos. If you can afford it, travel as much as possible. Whatever you do, don't give up. The minute you give up, you know you're not fit for *National Geographic*. It's sad but true – this is one career where quitting is never an option.

The lowdown

Education or qualifications: None, but tertiary studies in visual arts and photography would help.

Experience required: Experience shooting stills for magazines and books is essential. Experience shooting in a variety of outdoor environments is also beneficial.

Training: Photography courses are available all over the world.

Restrictions: Must be able to travel.

Negotiation consultant

If you have a natural knack for getting what you want and the killer instincts to rival that of a great white shark, then dedicating your life's work to helping others negotiate deals is a legitimate career path worth investigating.

It may sound like a made up job title (because it is) but negotiation consultants work with businesses and individuals to ensure their negotiations run smoothly and deliver the best outcomes. Covering everything from salary negotiations to the sale of commercial properties and crisis management, negotiation consultants know everything about the art of the deal back-to-front and inside-out.

Running their own enterprises, negotiation consultants have many different revenue streams. They might consult with firms to handle a one-off contract negotiation, deliver negotiation tactics workshops to corporate teams, or provide one-on-one negotiation training to individuals who want to feel empowered in their sales job. This is a career that can be taken in many different directions.

So what do you need to start your own negotiation consultancy? Well, the best thing about this job is that you don't necessarily need to devote yourself to years of tertiary study. Sure a degree in business or psychology would help, but it's by no means essential. If you were the type of kid who successfully managed to negotiate with your parents for an extra cookie or later bedtime, then bingo – you're exactly the type of person who could make it in this business.

Possessing pure, raw, unadulterated talent in getting what you want (without hurting anyone else) is the key here. And don't underestimate the 'not hurting anyone else' bit because negotiation works best when both parties feel like they've got a good deal. Rip someone off and they are less likely to play ball with you or recommend you to anyone else. So yeah, this negotiation thing is a lot harder than it looks.

If you're a professional negotiator the sky's the limit when it comes to income. If you're as good at your job as you say you are, then earning six figures shouldn't be a problem. Working with large corporations and high net worth individuals certainly puts professional negotiators in a good place to cultivate a reliable flow of income from doing what they love (and getting what they want).

The downsides to this career path mainly lie on the reputation management front. Many people are deadset frightened of negotiating and fear anyone who is good at it. Work hard to build bridges with clients and nail the 'confident but not cocky' vibe and the world is your (well-priced) oyster.

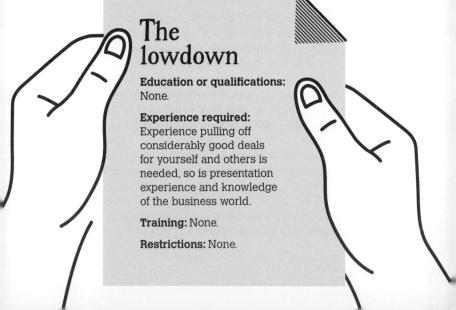

The lowdown

Education or qualifications: None.

Experience required: Experience pulling off considerably good deals for yourself and others is needed, so is presentation experience and knowledge of the business world.

Training: None.

Restrictions: None.

Panda handler

Do you often lose hours to watching cute animal videos on YouTube? Can you think of nothing better than dedicating your days to looking after some of the world's most adorable, and cheeky, creatures? Then the highly coveted role of panda handler might just be for you.

Often popping up on 'the best job in the world' lists, being a panda handler (or panda nanny) is the stuff dreams are made of. Zookeepers all over the world get to interact with pandas, but the plum roles go to the handlers employed by panda protection organisations, mostly located in rural China.

With numbers remaining quite precarious thanks to deforestation, it's estimated that there are little more than 1500 pandas remaining in the wild. Because of this, breeding programs have stepped up to try and save the species from extinction. And with the success of the breeding programs (yay!) comes the need for lots of precious, snuggly baby pandas to be loved and cared for.

In China, panda nannies provide round-the-clock care for newborn and infant pandas in research centres. This involves feeding, playing with and cleaning up after some of the most mischievous animals on earth. If you're not sure how much trouble a baby panda could cause, then look up baby panda videos online to see what the little balls of fluff are capable of. There are videos of baby pandas hiding in baskets, destroying items like mops and rakes, clinging onto the panda handlers en masse and creating all sorts of pandemonium (sorry – you weren't going to get to the end of this section without at least one panda pun).

But this job isn't all fun and games. The job of a panda nanny is a 24/7 affair. If there's a late-night panda emergency, then you're expected to respond with love and care. That's why panda nannies employed by Chinese research facilities are also given food and accommodation on top of their salary; such are the demands of the role, all panda nannies must live on site.

The isolated location of most panda research organisations in China means that this isn't a long-term career choice for most people. It's certainly a good way to break into animal handling, earn a solid income, contribute to the preservation of one of the world's most endangered (and ridiculously huggable) animals, and have one of the coolest job titles in the world. Imagine bumping into an old school friend and answering the inevitable 'What have you been doing with yourself lately?' question. 'Oh, just working with giant pandas in China. I did a stint as a panda nanny,' will be your answer. Cue extreme levels of street cred.

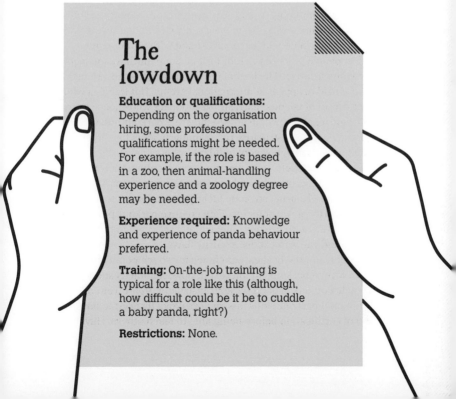

The lowdown

Education or qualifications: Depending on the organisation hiring, some professional qualifications might be needed. For example, if the role is based in a zoo, then animal-handling experience and a zoology degree may be needed.

Experience required: Knowledge and experience of panda behaviour preferred.

Training: On-the-job training is typical for a role like this (although, how difficult could be it be to cuddle a baby panda, right?)

Restrictions: None.

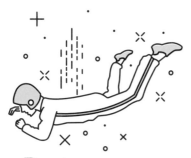

Parkour instructor

If the idea of working in a corporate role makes you want to take a running leap off a building, then you'll be pleased to know that there's a way to build a career out of running, jumping, flipping and vaulting yourself about the place. It's called parkour and if you're good enough, you can make a tidy living from teaching others this energetic activity that originated in France.

The dynamic art of navigating urban environments using your body in a series of mesmerising ways, parkour is characterised by climbing, jumping, rolling and swinging up, around and over buildings, staircases, concrete slabs, bridges and other urban structures most people just walk around without noticing.

Most people practise parkour for fun, but many have managed to turn it into a career. The best of the best perform stunts on movie sets and are paid to appear at international events. But there's a whole other subset of talented parkour practitioners who choose to spend their time teaching people how to integrate parkour into their lives.

Some parkour instructors run training schools to teach children and teens parkour in school holidays, others operate as one-on-one instructors for adults who are more serious about their training. Matt Damon was taught parkour lessons when preparing for his role as Jason Bourne, so some lucky parkour instructors get to work with celebrity movie stars too. One creative parkour practitioner even consults with prisons – he actually gets paid to break out of jail remand yards to expose security flaws.

Possibly not the best career choice for couch potatoes, anyone with a love of parkour, an interest in physical fitness and a desire to teach would be a good parkour instructor. Apart from having exceptional parkour skills, instructors typically need to have some level of certification before being able to teach others. Having good communication skills is also a must, as is having patience (you'll need to stay calm when little Timmy misses the mark for the hundredth time in a week).

Most parkour instructors run their own companies so it's important to have business acumen, marketing knowledge and customer service skills. As an activity that isn't exactly mainstream, much of your time will be spent letting people know about what you do and what physical and mental benefits parkour can have on children and adults.

Being able to run your own business is a huge benefit of this career, as nothing tastes better than sweet, sweet freedom. Moving your body every day is also a big plus, as you'll get to avoid the proven ill effects of sitting all day and working in offices without natural light and air flow. Oh, and if you're about to miss the bus you can just make a run for it, dramatically vaulting over trash cans and parked cars, and spring through the closing doors of the bus like the badass you know you are. All in a day's work for a parkour instructor.

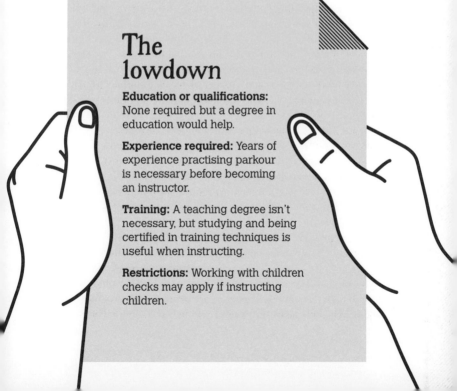

The lowdown

Education or qualifications: None required but a degree in education would help.

Experience required: Years of experience practising parkour is necessary before becoming an instructor.

Training: A teaching degree isn't necessary, but studying and being certified in training techniques is useful when instructing.

Restrictions: Working with children checks may apply if instructing children.

Penguin keeper

Do you prefer the company of animals to humans? Not afraid of getting a little dirty? Are you patient enough to cultivate an understanding of animal behaviour that is very different from your own? Then working in a zoo as a penguin keeper is the creative career perfect for you.

When it comes to adorable animal species, penguins are up there with the greats of the animal world. After all, what could be cuter than the sight of a bunch of baby penguins collectively losing their footing and slip-sliding all the way down an ice shelf? Yep, penguins are the cutest and are quite the drawcard in zoos and aquariums around the world.

Only found in the wild in certain parts of the world – Antarctica, Australia, New Zealand, Patagonia, South Africa, the Galapagos Islands – most of the rest of the planet has two options for seeing penguins: watching a David Attenborough documentary or heading to the zoo.

Penguin keepers are essentially zoo staff tasked with maintaining the welfare of the penguins housed within the zoo enclosure. Most get this rare, coveted job after studying zoology or animal behaviour science at a tertiary institution. So if you're thinking about this career path then start investing time in studying as this isn't the type of job they just give inexperienced people off the street (sorry).

An average day in the life of a penguin keeper involves making sure the penguins have enough food, adequate space to sleep, are free from disease and are not showing outward signs of distress. Ensuring that the animals are challenged and entertained is a big part of being a zookeeper, as confined animals can display mental and physical problems not present in their wild counterparts. So creating games and activities that simulate behaviour in the wild, for example, hunting and nesting, is a huge part of penguin keeping.

Some penguin keepers are involved in breeding programs and research projects, and almost all have to talk to zoo visitors and educate them on the lives of penguins and penguin behaviour. But back to the captive breeding ... I know your heart just skipped a beat at the thought of being in close proximity to baby penguins. So the answer is yes: penguin keepers get to hang out with baby penguins during breeding season.

Before you start thinking that this is truly the most magical profession of all, there are downsides to this role. Firstly, you have to be okay with getting dirty. While cute, penguins are still animals so the work isn't too glamorous. Another sad but inevitable part of the role is dealing with sick, injured or terminally ill penguins. So, while having compassion is a good thing, it's important to understand the circle of life and when it's time for some penguins to waddle over the rainbow bridge to penguin heaven, which I imagine is full of ice caves and delicious fish buffets.

Apart from the above pitfalls, in this role you'll avoid working with a bunch of suits in an office, and get to work with little birds wearing teeny, tiny matching tuxedos. If this isn't the very definition of living the dream, I don't know what is.

The lowdown

Education or qualifications: A zoology degree is generally required.

Experience required: Experience working with animals within a zoological setting is essential.

Training: Most zoos and aquariums have on-the-job training but to be a penguin keeper you should already have extensive knowledge of penguin behaviour and experience handling animals.

Restrictions: None.

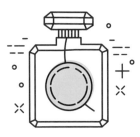

Perfumer

If the idea of bringing romance and happiness into the world in the form of good smells appeals to you, then why not follow your nose and pursue a career in perfumery?

Becoming part of a small industry that is notoriously difficult to break into, the life of a perfumer is certainly not all about floating around in a dreamy, fragrant world. Instead, it's a life dedicated to the surprisingly technical pursuit of capturing the unknown, then bottling it and marketing it to the masses. In other words: it's actually really hard work.

The road to becoming a perfumer is a long one. Many perfumers study chemistry in order to understand the compounds that make up a fragrance and learn how to mix them to create miracles. Some perfumers manage to learn this from a young age if they are exposed to the art of perfumery early on in their lives via an older family member. However, if your parents don't own a perfumery then studying chemistry is a good place to start.

A total obsession with fragrance is needed in order to excel in this career, as being able to pick up and then replicate the slightest of scents is essential. From floral bouquets reminiscent of frolicking in the fields in spring to earthy, woody aromas redolent of the forest floor, or fresh, fruity concoctions that speak of summer in Hawaii, perfumes have the mysterious ability to lift moods, allow people to time travel and cover up all manner of body odours. It's for this reason that perfumers are a little like magicians – they take chemical compounds and turn them into liquid gold.

So where can a perfumery take you? Some perfumers work for large fragrance houses, others run their own businesses selling directly to the public. While France is a hot spot for boutique perfumeries, independents can be found everywhere from Montreal to Melbourne. Selling perfumes, scented soaps and candles, some perfumers even work with clients to develop their own bespoke, signature scent.

This is quite a niche career choice, but with people using fragrance since the early days of civilisation, it isn't going anywhere anytime soon. People keen to pursue this aromatic career should be the hardworking and dedicated type as there is so much learning through trial and error in this business. If you're the type that gives up on things easily or can't stay focused, then perfumery will drive you up the wall. Even the most experienced of perfumers are often defeated when trying to create a specific fragrance, so you really need to be able to stay the course to see where your experiments end up.

There are many rewards that come with being a perfumer, and the greatest surely has to be creating a new fragrance that no one in the world has ever smelled before. With this in mind, perfumers are a little bit like mad scientists in pursuit of making the world smell great. A very worthy cause to dedicate your life to!

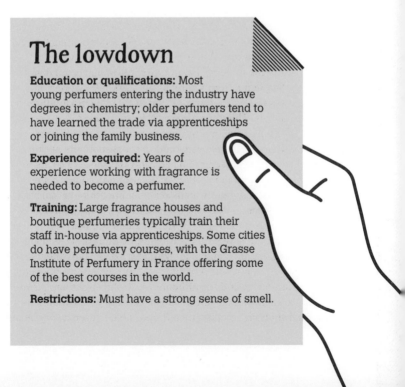

The lowdown

Education or qualifications: Most young perfumers entering the industry have degrees in chemistry; older perfumers tend to have learned the trade via apprenticeships or joining the family business.

Experience required: Years of experience working with fragrance is needed to become a perfumer.

Training: Large fragrance houses and boutique perfumeries typically train their staff in-house via apprenticeships. Some cities do have perfumery courses, with the Grasse Institute of Perfumery in France offering some of the best courses in the world.

Restrictions: Must have a strong sense of smell.

Personal shopper

If getting paid to spend other people's money on luxury items seems too good to be true, prepare to have your mind blown right apart by the world of personal shopping. The perfect career choice for good communicators with a love of fashion and an eye for a good buy, personal shopping is so much more than just going nuts at a department store while someone else foots the bill.

Usually hired by high net worth individuals who have little time to shop, personal shoppers spend their days sourcing items for their clients who don't mind paying top dollar to get someone else to do the running around. From finding the latest 'must have' Chanel pumps to securing a whole summer wardrobe for an upcoming Caribbean beach break, personal shoppers leave no stone unturned in the quest to fulfil their clients' (sometimes insatiable) retail desires.

But finding items from a list isn't all personal shoppers do – many also make suggestions and assist their clients to make the right purchases. That bejewelled red leather jacket may seem like a good idea when a client is going through a Nashville phase but what will it be worth next season? Personal shoppers are there to guide wayward clients out of bad wardrobe choices and steer them towards investment pieces they will wear for decades. Same goes with Christmas gifting. Christmas is the time for personal shoppers to shine – finding that sold-out must-have toy or rare vintage timepiece takes patience, persistence and inventiveness.

Many personal shoppers operate their own business and charge a consulting fee or retainer, but some high-end department stores and shopping centres also employ in-house personal shoppers to help customers to find the ultimate wardrobe or gift haul. If you choose to strike out on your own and develop your own freelance personal shopping empire, then it's possible to earn a very healthy living, especially if you nab a few celebrity clients with deep pockets and the ability to refer you on to their other cashed-up celeb friends. Some celebrities even pay for their personal shopper to accompany them to fashion shows in Paris and buying trips in London.

Even though being surrounded by luxury goods and mixing with celebrities are highlights of the job, one of the best parts of pursuing a personal shopping career is that almost any enterprising person with good people skills and an eye for a good buy can do it. There are no educational requirements or qualifications needed to position yourself as a personal shopper. Just simply research the retail scene, get to know your labels, stores and dealers, make connections within the retail sector, set up a website and start marketing yourself as the personal shopper you'd be crazy to spend money without.

Of course, you will have to deal with your fair share of nightmarish *The Devil Wears Prada*-type characters who will make you want to tear your hair out in rage, but you'll also get extreme satisfaction out of delivering that rare, first edition copy of *Pride and Prejudice* to your delighted (well-paying) client. Oh, and then there's the whole getting paid to spend other people's money thing. That's the sweetest part of all.

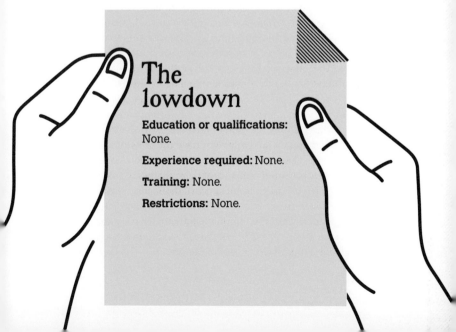

The lowdown

Education or qualifications: None.

Experience required: None.

Training: None.

Restrictions: None.

Pet nanny

If you believe that dogs are some of the best peeps you know and cats are worth bowing down to, then becoming a pet nanny will ensure you're constantly surrounded by your type of 'people' at work.

W.C. Fields once quipped 'never work with children or animals', but that hasn't stopped legions of people choosing to work with creatures every day. There are dog walkers and groomers, veterinarians and vet nurses, pet photographers, animal behaviour experts, animal rescue workers and people who breed and show pure-bred animals, as parodied in the hit movie *Best in Show*.

Once relegated to the backyard and fed food scraps, many dogs now live indoors and feast on organic meals before sleeping in the same bed as their owner each night. Felines haven't done too badly either, regularly chowing down on cat food varieties featuring premium ingredients and wearing diamanté-studded collars made by high-end fashion houses. The number of over-indulged pets being treated better than many humans on this planet is something that perplexes many. Despite this, it's a phenomenon that continues to grow, with pet nannies being a prime example of how far people will go to ensure the comfort and happiness of their furry family members.

Usually working from the home of the pet owner, a pet nanny stays with the pet/s while the owner is away on vacation or at work. The tasks of a pet nanny can include meal preparation, walks, cuddles, brushing sessions and medication dosing. Many pet nannies are paid to do nothing more than sit on the couch and watch television with a cat or two on their lap. Others are expected to take high-energy pooches to the beach or park for long runs and ball-chasing sessions. Sending updates to anxious owners via social media is sometimes another part of the job.

Most pet nannies are self-employed, although some are on the payroll of high net worth individuals like celebrities. While the income of a pet nanny fluctuates, it's considered a low-stress job that allows you to avoid working in offices and other formal, corporate environments. Forget power suits and pencil skirts – the average wardrobe of a pet nanny is sweatpants and comfy sneakers.

Pet nannies need to be prepared to get dirty, with picking up dog poop and cleaning out kitty litter trays the most unglamorous parts of the role. The job of a pet nanny may seem like a bit of a lark, but this vocation also comes with huge responsibility. Losing a dog during a walk or leaving the back door open for kitty to escape out of isn't a good look, so being careful and diligent is vital, especially when dealing with special needs or geriatric pets that require medication.

The perfect role for anyone who understands animal behaviour and is confident with handling pets of all kinds, being a pet nanny is a fun way to earn money. With plenty of on-the-job downtime (when Kitty or Fido are napping), it's the ideal role to take on when studying or pursuing another craft such as writing or drawing. Sure, you'll probably spend a lot of time talking to animals in this job, but when compared to many corporate roles, what's the difference?

The lowdown

Education or qualifications: No formal education requirements.

Experience required: Experience handling animals is highly recommended.

Training: None required. However, completing an animal handling course would help.

Restrictions: People who are allergic to cat and dog hair might want to rethink being a pet nanny. Some employers might require a police check before hiring. Having good physical fitness and the ability to walk long distances is required when minding large dogs.

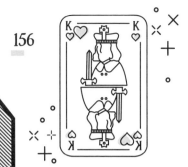

Poker player

Do you fancy yourself as a bit of card shark? Can you think of nothing better than dedicating your days to playing cards? Then stepping into the world of professional poker playing could be a career worth pursuing. Your parents probably aren't going to like it initially, but once you bring home a big, fat novelty cheque from your first tournament win, you can bet your bottom dollar they'll soon be bragging to all their friends about how talented you are.

Dominated by an elite few, the world of professional poker playing captivates many (and bemuses many others who think it's not a 'real job'). Whether it's the extreme amounts of prize money on offer, the glamorous trips to Las Vegas or the sheer chutzpah required to bluff your way to victory, the life of a pro poker player is one many people would love to live, even if just for a day.

While some poker players build a career out of playing small tournaments both locally and online, the big paydays (and fame) can be found on the professional circuit where large tournaments (and even larger cheques) dominate. How big does it get? Well, with some poker tournaments televised, poker is now also a spectator sport and with that comes television rights, endorsements and sponsorship deals. In that respect, poker playing is as legitimate as many mainstream sports.

To make it on the professional circuit you really need much, much more than a good poker face. You also need to have a watertight understanding of the rules of the game, nerves of steel and the supreme ability to read others. You need to be patient and be okay with a bit of trash talking to put everyone else off their game. Poker is a waiting game, with most players sitting around for hours watching others play, and lose, before striking at the right moment.

So playing hand after hand is a requirement, and this is where boredom can set in if you don't really love the game.

Possessing a good understanding of mathematics is helpful, but arguably the best thing you can do for yourself if you want to be a poker pro is play hours and hours and hours of poker. In this field, personal experience is everything and it can't be found in a book or on YouTube. As a career that crushes anyone stupid or naive enough to think they know it all, dedicating a serious amount of time to developing your skills will put you in the best position to succeed and not end up living on the boulevard of broken dreams. As a highly stressful career, this isn't the right fit for anyone who wants a guaranteed stable income or low-risk life. However, if you love the thrill of playing cards, are happy to travel to tournaments and have strong poker skills, then it could be for you.

On top of the prize money, some of the best players also earn extra income from endorsements with companies like Pepsi, Chrysler and Puma, who have all sponsored players in the past. With multi-million dollar paydays on offer, all you need is one good tournament to be set for life – if you don't fold too soon.

The lowdown

Education or qualifications: None.

Experience required: Experience playing poker in a high-stakes environment is a must. This experience will give you the ability to read other people's body language and handle the intense pressure of the game.

Training: None. Just years of playing poker. Although there are also poker courses, books and online tutorials to help.

Restrictions: None. Unless you get caught cheating and end up getting thrown out of the circuit or blacklisted from casinos.

Political decoy

Now here's a job that is so damn strange you probably won't be able to tell anyone about it because it will blow their tiny minds to smithereens (and potentially compromise national security in the process).

As one of the most mysterious, and rare, jobs in the world, political decoys are employed by the government to impersonate a political figurehead, head of state or other VIP in order to keep them out of danger. After an important public address, you might drive away in one limousine while the speech-giver legs it out the back door in another limousine. This is how political decoys work. It may sound like something out of a spy novel written in the 1960s, but it's safe to say that political decoys are still employed by many governments around the world.

With so much mystery and intrigue surrounding this type of work it's hard to identify anyone working in this field, but they must be out there. Hitler used a political decoy and Boris Yeltsin was also rumoured to use decoys, as did Saddam Hussein. Basically any well-known, controversial figurehead at risk of being killed could be using a decoy right now.

The only way to get this type of work is to have a strong physical resemblance to a person of great importance, so most of the population are immediately knocked out of the running. But if you look in the mirror and see Donald Trump smiling back, then you could turn that into a money spinner and fashion yourself a career as a Donald Double.

Political decoy work is a tough ask, though. Sure, you get to travel the world, perhaps even seeing the inside of Downing Street, Air Force One, The Hague or the White House, but ultimately this type of anxiety-inducing work is dangerous. It's not a stretch to say that you could be shot in an assassination attempt gone wrong, so before stepping into a decoy role, you'll need to be okay with putting your life on the line for your country. You may be asked to alter your physical appearance with make-up, wigs, even scarification, all in the pursuit of looking exactly like the person you're impersonating.

Without the ability to tell your family and friends what you do for a living, you'll have to be a master manipulator to wriggle your way out of all those 'So, what do you do for a living?' conversations and the 'Where the hell have you been for the past three weeks?' questions. But if you're borderline sociopathic, cool with lying to your nearest and dearest, and happen to have strong physical resemblance to say, the President of the USA, then you're in luck.

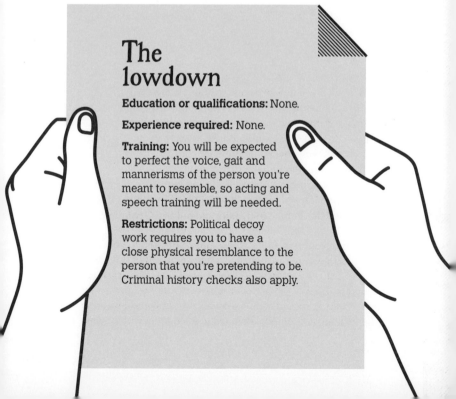

The lowdown

Education or qualifications: None.

Experience required: None.

Training: You will be expected to perfect the voice, gait and mannerisms of the person you're meant to resemble, so acting and speech training will be needed.

Restrictions: Political decoy work requires you to have a close physical resemblance to the person that you're pretending to be. Criminal history checks also apply.

Puppeteer

The perfect career choice for anyone who is hell bent on not growing up, puppeteers create and work with puppets to put together performances that bring joy, laughter (and sometimes terror) to the lives of children and adults all over the world.

From Elmo to Kermit the Frog; Lamb Chop; Sooty, Sweep and Soo; and Chucky from *Child's Play*, puppets have entertained us on stage and screen for centuries. Digital animation may have changed the entertainment industry forever, but puppets still have an important place in comedy, TV, films and theatre.

These days the art of puppeteering has moved on from the lo-fi street stylings of the Punch and Judy show held in the town square of a village. Increasingly, puppeteers are working in the animatronics field. Anima-what? Animatronics is basically the science of making puppets that have been wired up to move and sometimes even talk on their own, not unlike robotics. Instead of using their hands to animate the puppet, technology is used to create movement. Not all puppeteers work in this field, but it's important to note that a career in puppeteering will, in all likelihood, include animatronics in the future.

Working on a wide range of productions including musicals, children's television shows, pantomimes and films, puppeteers must have a specific combination of skills and talents in order to thrive in the puppeteering world. Sure, the ability to build cool puppets is up there, but performance is a huge element of this job, so being able to read and write scripts is essential, as is having a broad understanding of the performing arts world. As a form of acting, puppeteering requires showmanship, great communication skills and a knack for comedy. Being able to connect with audiences (without them actually ever seeing you) isn't easy and is the kind of rare, weird skill that is cultivated over years of practice.

If you're unsure of how successful puppeteering can be, look to the career of Jim Henson for some inspiration. The creator of The Muppets led a wildly successful life, managing to turn his love of puppets into a multifaceted and highly profitable career. Although not everyone can reach the dizzying heights of Jim Henson, puppeteers can be found working at children's birthday parties, on theatre stages, film sets and television studios.

Still, puppeteering roles are few and far between, so you'd want to really, really, really love puppets to pursue this career. Job security is rare in this business; therefore being able to market yourself and connect with the key players in the entertainment industry is essential. Some puppeteers supplement their income by building puppets for others, so there are various ways to secure several income streams if you're clever and industrious enough to both build and perform.

Hitting the big time may be rare, but when you're a puppeteer you get to give birth to new characters, make people smile and laugh, have fun with your work and bring huge amounts of joy to the world. Now how many investment bankers can say that about their jobs?

The lowdown

Education or qualifications: No official education requirements, although a degree in performing arts would be helpful.

Experience required: Experience building and working with puppets, as well as acting and performing is generally required.

Training: Most puppeteers learn the art in performing arts or specialised puppetry schools.

Restrictions: Working with children and criminal record checks are required to work with children.

Reader

Word nerds unite! If you're the type of person who is often found lurking in libraries and bookshops then you'll be pleased to know that it is possible to earn money while indulging your love of the written word. Professional reading is a thing and could just be a cool way to work in the publishing industry without being a writer.

With publishers receiving thousands of unsolicited manuscripts each year, professional readers are a necessary cog in the wheel of the publishing business. Tasked with wading through the slush pile to find the literary gems hidden within, readers use their knowledge and experience to make recommendations on whether the manuscripts show potential.

Writing a detailed report on the manuscript, a reader must have a good grip on the essentials of the book publishing business, including the importance of good plotting, character development, dialogue, story arc and what types of books sell like hotcakes.

Discovering the next bestseller is the intent, however, in reality readers actually spend much of their time trawling through real stinkers. From critiquing poorly written robot-sex genre fiction to dealing with obvious rip-offs of the latest publishing fad (not another *50 Shades of Grey* imitation, please), professional readers are charged with the task of finding the lotus blooming in the swamp.

Many professional readers start out working within the publishing industry as interns or publisher's assistants. Going through an editor's sizeable slush pile is a good way to get a handle on what is required of professional manuscript readers. Other professional readers have a background in publishing either as writers or editors.

Many readers work on a freelance basis, so this career offers freedom and flexibility. Depending on your needs or personal situation, you can take the work as fast or slow as needed. Want to work part time to have a baby? Then simply take on fewer manuscripts. Want to make more money and put in extra hours? Then let publishers know you want to take on more reading. Some people even take on this career as a side hustle while working on other projects (like writing their own novel).

Having a good grasp on language is essential, as is understanding the publishing industry and being abreast of industry trends. Being able to offer constructive criticism while setting aside your own bias is also key. The most important attribute a reader could have is a passion for reading. If you don't love books or don't want to live a life surrounded by words, then you're on a hiding to nothing with this role!

Professional reading may not sound like a high-octane career, however, you could be responsible for spotting the next J. K. Rowling. On the flipside, you could also be responsible for *passing* on the next J. K. Rowling. This is truly high-stakes reading.

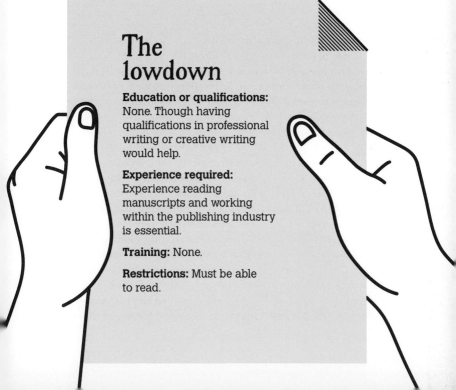

The lowdown

Education or qualifications: None. Though having qualifications in professional writing or creative writing would help.

Experience required: Experience reading manuscripts and working within the publishing industry is essential.

Training: None.

Restrictions: Must be able to read.

Screenwriter

A good career option for anyone who has ever watched a soap opera and thought, 'Who the hell comes up with this crap? I could write better storylines than this', screenwriting provides an opportunity to shape and create works that have the ability to enlighten, entertain and sometimes enrage viewers.

Surely the dream profession of any hardcore cinema or television buff with a love of the written word, screenwriting is one of those careers that many people would love to pursue but feel is out of their reach. While certainly not a profession for just anyone, it is entirely possible to make a good living from screenwriting, particularly if you are in a position to move to Hollywood where thousands of the world's screenwriters live and work.

For a professional screenwriter, there's an astounding array of places to apply your talent. From cheesy, made-for-television Christmas movies to big-budget sci-fi flicks and animated features, there are many genres to explore when working in screenwriting. Apart from film, screenwriters also work on commercials and television series and, with the recent explosion in high-quality television drama, many argue that writing for television is now the place to be. Even video game designers require the input of a screenwriter to bring their stories to life.

The best part of this profession is that there are many ways to get there. Some successful screenwriters attended screenwriting classes in college, others have no higher education and picked up the trade by working in the business and learning from senior scriptwriters. Attending a screenwriting course can only help your career prospects, but it's certainly not the only way to get a foot in the door.

From plotting a riveting story arc to writing killer dialogue, the art of screenwriting isn't as easy as it sounds. Many screenwriters work on a freelance basis, meaning that they can go from rags to riches (and sometimes rags again) depending on the project. And there's the hard work, long hours and crippling self-doubt involved in birthing any kind of monumental creative endeavour.

Because screenwriting is a collaborative process, much of your time is spent dealing with other people. Most screenwriters are hired to work on a specific production, so they are beholden to the whims of others (unless you're Quentin Tarantino, then you can do whatever you damn well like). Whether screenwriters are working with a team of other writers, or working with an author to take a book from print to screen, or listening to unsavoury feedback from an actor who wants their dialogue rewritten, screenwriters have little control over their work. Scenes you toiled over end up on the cutting room floor, characters you created are killed off because producers don't like them and scenes are rewritten to please directors.

Apart from being astonishingly good creative writers with an inherent understanding of film and television, screenwriters must also be patient and proactive. For those fortunate enough to make it to the top, there's the opportunity to work on award-winning films, walk the red carpet at film premieres and meet and work with film and TV legends. A fair trade for having a scene or two cut now and then? You decide.

The lowdown

Education or qualifications: None, although screenwriting courses and college modules are taught all over the world and online. Despite this, a tertiary education isn't required to be a successful screenwriter.

Experience required: Knowledge of or experience working in the film industry is helpful.

Training: Screenwriting courses are available, although working with more senior screenwriters is a good way to receive on-the-job training.

Restrictions: None.

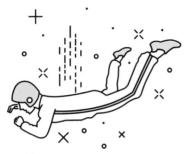

Skydiving instructor

Do you like to live on the edge? Can you think of nothing better than getting paid to scare the wits out of people each and every day? Do you often have dreams that you can fly? Then make those dreams a reality by becoming a skydiving instructor. It will really annoy your parents but the views alone are worth it.

Jumping out of an airplane for a living must surely rate as one of the most hardcore careers to emerge in modern times. With many people having an insatiable thirst for adventure, recreational skydiving has really taken off in the last few decades, paving the way for a whole crop of people to make money out of it.

Instructing others how to jump and then land safely after exiting an airplane located thousands of metres in the air isn't for everyone. As a highly specialised career path, in many ways skydiving instructors need to have split personalities. On one hand they need to have a wild, insatiable thirst for adventure, but on the other they need to be serious and responsible enough to adhere to safety regulations. One part Bodhi from *Point Break*, one part hall monitor, skydiving instructors need to calm the nervous energy of their students while telling them to jump out of a freaking plane. It's a tightrope walk of a life, and one only suited to certain types of people.

People only get to become skydiving instructors after years of practice. You can't take a few jumps then be given a role teaching others. Instructors must be certified and have completed many types of courses. Covering everything from first aid application to dealing with crisis situations, assessing weather patterns, packing parachutes correctly and handling difficult people, skydiving instructors are multi-talented folk.

With skydiving instructors operating on most continents in the world (sorry Antarctica, no skydiving for you), this career path could really take you places. The pay isn't exactly huge, but if you ran your own skydiving school you could potentially grow a nice nest egg over the years. Regardless, skydiving isn't something you get into for the money. If skydivers loved money more than they loved the rush of freefalling through the air at top speeds, then they all would have become futures traders. No, skydiving instructors tend to value other things more than cold hard cash. This is one profession that is all about chasing thrills, being at one with the universe, enjoying the outdoors and taking (calculated) risks in the name of adventure. And what could be better than teaching newcomers this philosophy? What could be better than waking up every working day knowing that in a few hours you'll be high up above it all, looking down on all those chumps working in office buildings?

The lowdown

Education or qualifications: No degree necessary but you must be certified to be a skydiving instructor.

Experience required: Hundreds of hours of experience in skydiving are required before becoming an instructor. Previous experience in teaching or instructing others is helpful.

Training: A minimum number of hours spent training is required. This depends on which country you work in and what type of instructor you are.

Restrictions: Must be physically and mentally fit.

Skywriter

Do you love to fly but hate the thought of joining the military or living the life of a perennially jet-lagged long-haul commercial pilot? If you're looking for a sign about which career to pursue, then look to the heavens because skywriting might just be for you.

From advertising brands of ice cream to emblazoning marriage proposals, skywriters all over the world take to the skies to bring messages to the masses. Hitting the scene in England back in the 1920s, skywriting was reportedly invented by a World War One veteran who recruited ex-pilots and taught them the art of flying planes not for dropping bombs, but to write messages in the sky for paying advertisers.

The ideal job for a pilot who doesn't want to commit to being in the military or being overseas for long periods of time, skywriters tend to work in one city, only working during the day (because no one has invented glow-in-the-dark skywriting vapours yet). Yes, skywriters have the best of both worlds in that they get to experience the thrill of flying regularly, but can go home to their own beds each and every night, jet-lag free.

Most skywriters tend to run their own businesses so, apart from having the ability to operate an aircraft and the technical know-how to use a small airplane to form letters and words in the sky, skywriters need to have the business acumen required to run a for-profit enterprise. A commitment to safety is also essential, as is the ability to adhere to aviation and environmental regulations.

Once all the above is covered, the fun stuff can happen. Soaring up into the sky to make shapes with vapour pouring out of the plane, skywriters write messages with an unbelievable amount of precision and accuracy. Writing a message upside down and back-to-front thousands of metres off the ground requires a steady hand, calm outlook and a commitment to quality. Cutting corners just won't work in this profession. In fact, cutting corners could result in a fatal accident, so only the most responsible and diligent of people can take on this type of role.

Running a skywriting business isn't a walk in the park considering how niche the industry is, but with large companies usually possessing huge budgets for advertising, skywriters can grab a piece of the pie if they're able to market themselves well. Sure, television, radio, print and online advertising may have scuttled the golden age of skywriting, but the novelty factor of trying to guess what the word or message will be, still captivates onlookers below almost a hundred years after the art of skywriting appeared.

Many people might be perplexed by the life of a skywriter, but the best part surely has to be having the ability to take to the skies and write messages seen by thousands – perhaps even smack downs to people who laugh at your career choice?

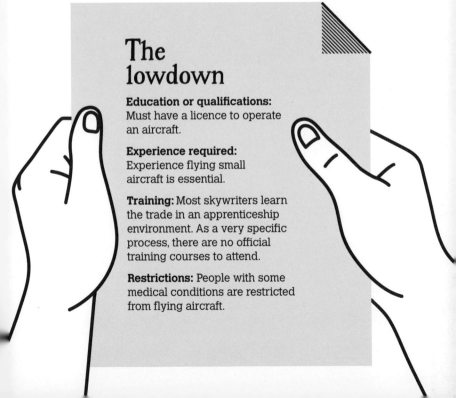

The lowdown

Education or qualifications: Must have a licence to operate an aircraft.

Experience required: Experience flying small aircraft is essential.

Training: Most skywriters learn the trade in an apprenticeship environment. As a very specific process, there are no official training courses to attend.

Restrictions: People with some medical conditions are restricted from flying aircraft.

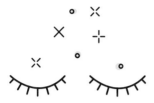

Sleeper

Is your bed one of your favourite places? Do you hit the snooze button with alarming frequency? Have you been known to turn a quick power nap into a coma-like sleep marathon? Then perhaps you could carve out a career as a professional sleeper. No, you're not dreaming, there are people in this world who are paid to sleep.

Pro sleepers are usually hired on a contractual or project basis by a variety of organisations and companies that require sleepers for a range of different reasons. Professional sleepers are paid to participate in scientific sleep studies, test out mattresses, trial sleep remedies and assess the comfort-level of hotel rooms and bedding. NASA even once hired people to stay in bed for just over two months in order to assess the impact of microgravity on the human body. Yes, a group of people got paid to stay in bed for two months!

Although it's probably not a suitable full-time career for most of the population, pro sleeping represents a good opportunity for people to supplement their income on a regular basis (and catch a lot of z's in the process). Of course, professional sleeping isn't all about having wicked flying dreams and drooling on pillows. Professional sleepers are expected to work. Whether it's filling out a report on how comfortable a hotel bed was, or reporting the side effects of sleep medication, or having wires and nodes hooked up to your body while you sleep, professional sleeping is definitely considered work and that's why people are compensated for it.

In short, professional sleepers are heroes who walk among us for they have managed to make money from going to bed. While the hapless inhabitants of the world are dragging themselves out of their beds in the morning to go to a dead-end job they loathe, pro sleepers are happily sharing their talent for extreme kipping and getting paid for it. *slow clap*

The lowdown

Education or qualifications: None.

Experience required: None.

Training: None.

Restrictions: Insomniacs need not apply. Some scientific studies may have strict selection criteria.

Smokejumper

Do you like to live on the edge? Does the idea of sitting at a desk in a beige office building for the rest of your life crush your spirit? Are you unafraid of the following things: heights, fires, isolation and intense bursts of physical activity? Yes? Then a career as a smokejumper could just be for you!

Combining parachuting with firefighting to create the mother of all terrifying jobs, smokejumping involves flinging yourself out of a light aircraft directly into a wildfire burning in a remote, hard-to-access forest with the purpose of extinguishing it before it spreads.

Considered the commandos of the firefighting world, smokejumpers must pass a series of rigorous, soul-crushing tests to gain the role. Let's put it this way: you must really, really, really want to jump straight into a hellfire in the middle of nowhere in order to pass.

The Russian Federation and the USA both have a long history of employing smokejumpers. They have been hiring and training these elite firefighters since the 1930s.

With more than 270 male and female smokejumpers currently employed by the United States Forest Service, smokejumpers complete a number of demanding physical and mental tests in order to qualify to jump out of planes into infernos. Many people hope to be smokejumpers, but only a small amount of rookies make it, such is the brutal nature of the training and, ultimately, the job. A regime of military-style physical exercises including running, push-ups, pull-ups and sit-ups are just the beginning of the program. Designed to build mental strength and weed out inappropriate candidates, rookie programs also involve mock airplane exits, learning how to use chainsaws, compass navigation exercises, emergency first aid training and many intense parachute-landing drills.

While certainly not one of the safest careers to pursue, the work of a smokejumper is one of the most adventurous ways to serve the community and make a real difference to the lives of others. It's the type of job that will see you forever apologising to your parents for signing up, but on the flipside, they'll also be forever proud of their badass smokejumping child.

The lowdown

Education or qualifications: No formal education requirements.

Experience required: As a specialised branch of firefighting, it takes years of experience as a firefighter to be considered for a smokejumping role.

Training: After qualifying and serving as a firefighter, smokejumpers must pass a series of physical and mental tests in order to qualify. Training involves everything from cargo retrieval to tree climbing, application of first aid and performing parachute-landing rolls. People can be dropped from the training program at any stage if they fail to meet any of the requirements.

Restrictions: Height and weight restrictions apply. People with certain medical conditions are ineligible to be smokejumpers.

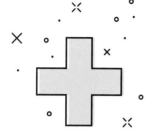

Snake milker

Pop quiz: Would you prefer to spend your days working with a bunch of investment bankers or a bunch of venomous snakes? Of course, that's a trick question because they are essentially the same thing. Pot shots at the bankers working at the top end of town aside, working with venomous snakes is a career possibility, with snake milking being one of the more interesting, and useful, ways to interact with snakes for a living.

Snake venom is used to create anti-venom for the treatment of bite victims. Laboratories and snake farms work together to cultivate a regular supply of venom in order to supply pharmaceutical companies and public health departments with the venoms used in snake-bite treatments.

As you suspected, getting the venom out of a highly poisonous, dangerous snake isn't the easiest of tasks and is only suited to highly experienced individuals. Snake milking is a delicate process that involves getting a snake to bite a jar covered with a latex lid. That bite will release venom into the jar, which will then be frozen, stored and shipped to a lab for processing. After that it will save someone's life so, yeah, no biggie right?

Safety is a huge part of this role, as is ensuring that snakes aren't milked too often because this creates problems with venom flow. Understanding snake behaviour is paramount, with following processes and adhering to policies around safety, hygiene and best practice snake milking being incredibly important. By now, you probably understand that this role is less about snake charming and more about cold, hard science. As such, snake milkers usually need experience working in labs.

Snake handling experience and certification is the most important credential required to fulfil this role. And if you don't really like being in close quarters with snakes, then snake milking is obviously not your thing. Living in a country with a high amount of venomous snakes is an advantage for this profession (high fives to all the Indian, Australian, South African, Brazilian, American and sub-Saharan readers).

Clearly not a role for everyone, snake milking is a career path perfect for people who love our scaly, deadly friends commonly associated with the devil and all things ominous. If you choose to dedicate yourself to snake milking, people may think you're a weirdo, but essentially every single day you will be helping to save people's lives and that's a whole lot more than most people can say they accomplish in an entire lifetime. Plus, you can avoid the fate of being an investment banker (who, ironically enough, will all meet a pit of snakes once they end up in hell for the Global Financial Crisis).

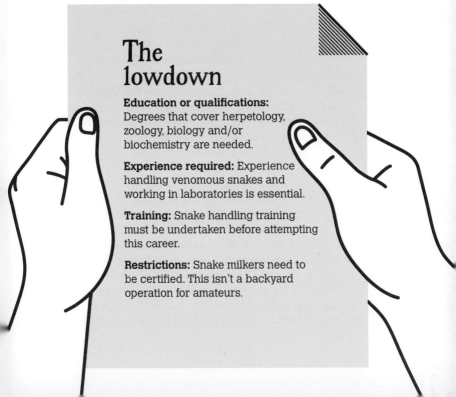

The lowdown

Education or qualifications:
Degrees that cover herpetology, zoology, biology and/or biochemistry are needed.

Experience required: Experience handling venomous snakes and working in laboratories is essential.

Training: Snake handling training must be undertaken before attempting this career.

Restrictions: Snake milkers need to be certified. This isn't a backyard operation for amateurs.

Spacesuit design engineer

Want a career path that will blow the minds of everyone you meet? If you're interested in engineering and design, and are a little bit obsessed with space, then you can do no better than designing the number one choice of clothing for astronauts. Yes, spacesuit design engineering might sound a little intimidating, but invest a few good years in graduate studies and you could find yourself working on a spacesuit worn by someone on Mars.

One of the coolest places any science graduate could end up working after spending years hitting the books and sweating over exam results is a space agency like NASA. And of all the jobs going at NASA, designing space suits has to be up there as one of the most interesting. Working in a large team of engineers, spacesuit designers develop spacesuits so future generations may be able to walk on Mars, move with more freedom around the International Space Station, and safely spacewalk in style.

Taking into account a mindboggling amount of intricate, critical factors, spacesuit design engineers have a killer combination of raw intelligence, a good work ethic, the ability to think with logic, and a supreme amount of engineering knowledge. Apart from having the technical skills to work on spacesuit design, engineers must be able to work in teams and communicate well with others. Writing complex reports is a huge part of the job, so possessing good writing skills is also useful.

Want to be a spacesuit engineer but don't know where to start? Well, start paying attention in mathematics and physics classes as you'll need to get extraordinarily good grades in both to progress to tertiary studies in aerospace engineering. With only the very best of the best selected to work at NASA, so-so candidates just won't make the cut. And rightly so, considering the high-stakes nature of space exploration. Spacesuits aren't just for comfort; they are a vehicle in themselves – wired up for communications, fitted with safety systems designed to preserve the life of astronauts and to enable them to pull off mission-critical tasks.

With very few roles available and years of study required to even get a chance at an internship with a space agency, spacesuit design engineering is a career for the very lucky few. But don't let that intimidate you or put you off – it's not rocket science (except it kind of is).

The lowdown

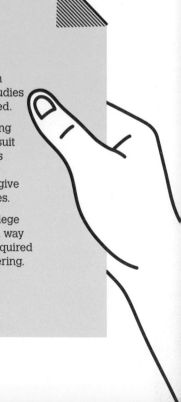

Education or qualifications: A degree in engineering is essential. Postgraduate studies in space science are also usually required.

Experience required: Experience working for space agencies is essential to spacesuit design. Experience designing spacesuits doesn't come easy though and is mostly attained through programs designed to give experience to new engineering graduates.

Training: NASA runs internships for college students and graduates. This is the ideal way to gain the highly specialised training required to work in spacesuit design and engineering.

Restrictions: Security clearance checks are required.

Speechwriter

Fancy penning a speech that could change the course of history? No pressure, of course, but if you've got a knack for persuasive writing and a healthy interest in geopolitics then trying your hand at speechwriting might be a good career move that could pay off in unexpected ways.

From Martin Luther King Junior's influential 'I have a dream' speech, to Winston Churchill's rousing 'We shall fight on the beaches' address, speeches have the tremendous power to change minds, bring tears to eyes, fortify nations and bring hope in times of need. In the case of poorly written speeches, they have the power to put people to sleep. Which is why speechwriting is so important. Anyone who has ever sat (or dozed) through a real humdinger of a bad speech knows speechwriters are worth their weight in gold.

The ideal job for someone with decent writing skills, an interest in politics and world affairs and a gift for communicating complicated messages in a simple way, speechwriting can be found in the political arena, although there is also a need for speechwriters within the corporate and not-for-profit sectors.

The life of a speechwriter can be exhilarating, especially when working on pivotal speeches for key figures. But on the flipside, burnout is common with this profession as the pace is often relentless and the content can sometimes be repetitive. Writing speeches isn't exactly easy, so that's why speechwriters are usually paid quite well for their efforts.

Some speechwriters work on a freelance basis, others work as staffers within government agencies. Either way, a good speechwriter has to have many skills above and beyond the actual writing. Being able to work in a team is essential, as speechwriting doesn't happen in a vacuum. Speechwriters need to be able to turn complex information and messages into compelling statements that people can instantly understand. As such, a good speechwriter will have a strong handle on global and social issues, and be able to provide a speech that matches the objectives of the person or agency requiring the speech. Going rogue just isn't a good idea for a speechwriter who wants a long career.

So apart from earning a good living and working with high-profile individuals, what else can a speechwriter reap from their profession? Some speechwriters also get to travel frequently – especially if working with heads of state – and the best of the best get to write speeches that are listened to over and over again, for decades to come. While you don't get paid per play, the satisfaction of knowing you were behind a speech that made people cry or change their viewpoint is surely worth more than mere money, right?

The lowdown

Education or qualifications: Most speechwriting roles require a degree in journalism, creative writing or media. Studies in politics are also helpful for political speechwriting roles.

Experience required: Experience in professional writing essential. Political speechwriting roles also require experience working in government roles.

Training: Speechwriting modules are often taught as part of writing and communications degrees. Speechwriting workshops and courses also exist.

Restrictions: Speechwriting roles with government departments might be subject to background checks.

Spoken word poet

Now here is a career guaranteed to ring the alarm bells of parents and friends obsessed with things like job security, earning power and benefits. Lucky they have their own lives to live and have no right interfering in yours. If you have a way with words and something important to say, then by all means, get up on your soapbox and pursue the wildly creative life of a spoken word poet.

Writing and performing poetry in person at bars, cafes, concert halls, bookshops and other spaces, spoken word poets, or slam poets, are independent artists who entertain, bemuse, thrill and provide inspiration. Gifted with an ability to connect with others through their words, spoken word poets revolutionised the world of poetry. Other forms of writing and entertainment rose to prominence with the introduction of the television and radio, and poetry was left on the shelf for decades until a few key players breathed new life into the historic medium in the sixties and seventies. Live performance of poetry made a resurgence in these decades thanks to poetry cafes popping up in cultural hot spots like New York. Combining elements of comedy, hip-hop and freestyle rap, poetry made a serious comeback.

With poetry slam competitions now held everywhere from Melbourne to Montreal, people are coming to spoken word poetry from a wide range of backgrounds and education levels. If you've got the gift of the gab, the confidence to perform live and the imagination required to pen new material that moves and inspires people, then spoken word poetry could be for you. There's no need for a Harvard degree or qualifications from a performing arts school; spoken word poetry is an art that can be perfected by almost anyone.

Of course, there will be plenty of naysayers, doubters and people who just don't understand your career path, but this is one of those professions where you have to say 'screw it' to convention and just go for it with all your energy. The best way to get into the game is to watch the greats, read the greats and practise, practise, practise. Read poetry books, attend poetry performances, be a part of the scene, drink it all up and then unleash your best on the world.

So how do poets make money anyway? Having the ability to hustle like your life depended on it is a huge part of being a successful working poet. Poets can make money in a variety of ways. From ticket sales for live performances to earning money from writing poetry for magazines, to printing your own poetry books and facilitating slam poetry workshops in schools, colleges and even prisons, an income *can* be earned from poetry. Of course, marketing and promotional skills are needed in order to make it, so is the ability to network with people in the industry.

The life of an independent artist is never an easy one, but it's guaranteed to be interesting. So do you want an easy life or an interesting life? If you chose the latter then spoken word poetry could be the right path for you.

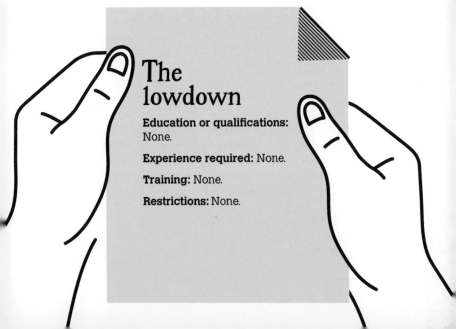

The lowdown

Education or qualifications: None.

Experience required: None.

Training: None.

Restrictions: None.

Sports psychologist

Hello sports fans; here's a job for you. Do you think you have what it takes to assist the world's best athletes to improve their performance? Are you a bit of a sports nut who is also interested in human behaviour? Then the action-packed world of sports psychology might be just the ticket.

All around the world, massive amounts of resources are poured into ensuring athletes and sports teams are successful. From the sunburnt cricket pitches of Australia to the hallowed outfield of Boston's Fenway Park and the well-manicured golf courses of Great Britain, teams of specialists are hired to support the careers of professional athletes. These days, you'd probably be hard-pressed to find an elite sportsperson who hasn't enlisted the help of a sports psychologist.

Along with a team of coaches, masseurs, doctors and nutritionists, sports psychologists work closely with athletes to help them consistently compete at the highest level. As one of the more exciting branches of psychology, sports psychology is the ideal career for someone who wants to combine their book smarts with their love of sports (yes, those two things can coexist).

Helping top athletes deal with the mental demands of constant training and competing is surely a dream job for any sports fan. Just knowing that you've played a small part in a comeback victory, a gold medal win, or a new personal best or world record makes this one career with a high job satisfaction rating. Imagine being the sports psychologist that helped lead the Chicago Cubs to their historic World Series win in 2016. Or, if you like your clients to be a little more demanding, imagine being the sports psychologist for former serial-racquet smasher and all-round tennis circuit bad boy, John McEnroe.

Of course, sports psychology isn't all about getting courtside seats and VIP access at Wimbledon. Charged with helping athletes keep calm during high-pressure moments, deal with the weight of expectations, cope with form slumps, manage a tough tour schedule, and transition through to retirement gracefully, sports psychologists must handle many challenging moments (and people) with professionalism and pragmatism.

In return for many years of serious study, sports psychologists are rewarded with an exciting career that attracts a high salary and allows interaction with some of the greatest names in the world of sports. Frequent travel is often involved and, for the top sports psychologists, there is the chance to take part in iconic events such as the Olympics or FIFA World Cup. Oh, and the free tickets, there's that too.

The lowdown

Education or qualifications: Minimum of a Masters or Doctorate degree in Psychology, plus additional study in the field of sports psychology.

Experience required: You should be undertaking studies of, or working with, professional sportspeople in a high-performance coaching environment.

Training: After qualifying as a psychologist, certain schools and colleges offer further study in order to become an accredited sports psychologist. This varies from country to country.

Restrictions: Most countries require an extensive criminal record check in order to qualify and be accredited as a psychologist. Some criminal histories may disqualify people from becoming a registered psychologist.

Sports statistician

Proving that a career in mathematics is anything but boring, the life of a sports statistician is both exciting, creative and, in some cases, quite lucrative. The dream job of any gifted mathlete who also happens to love competitive sports, crunching the numbers to help teams to greatness is a plum job well worth pursuing if you have the ability.

As demonstrated in the Academy Award-nominated film *Moneyball*, using statistics to get an edge over the competition can result in huge payoffs. Athletes can train as much as they like, receive motivational talks, consult with doctors, wear the latest high-performance gear and follow innovative diets, but sometimes the difference between a win or a loss can be due to the better use of statistics.

As such, more and more elite-level teams are employing sports statisticians to run the numbers in order to make better decisions when developing game plans and selecting teams. From baseball to cricket, football and beyond, sports statisticians influence almost every professional sports game broadcast on television.

A solid career choice for statistics professionals with a love of sports, most professional sporting teams hire statisticians to work with them full time or to consult with the team for a period of time. Most statisticians have degrees in mathematics or have studied statistics at a high level. Professional statisticians also have technical knowledge of computer programs used in generating statistical reports and advanced understanding of statistical methods used in the business. Suffice to say, if you don't know what the Monte Carlo method is then you're out of your depth in this profession.

The payoffs in following this career path are many. Statisticians are usually well paid, but working in the sports field amplifies the remuneration, especially if working for a high profile team. Of course, working with a team of elite sporting professionals is a highly enviable position to be in, with free access to sold-out games and getting to meet some of the greatest athletes in the world rating high on the envy meter. But most of all, being able to stick it to everyone who bullied you at school for loving numbers is the ultimate victory (as is being the mathematical genius behind a Super Bowl win).

The lowdown

Education or qualifications: A degree in mathematics or other relevant qualifications in statistics is required.

Experience required: Experience working with sports teams in some capacity is helpful. Having experience working in statistics in other fields is also useful.

Training: Taking on a role as a statistician with an elite sports team generally means your training days are over. Many statisticians gain on-the-job training in the field by voluntarily working with local or college sports teams.

Restrictions: None.

Storm chaser

There are two types of people in this world: those who watch the nineties action flick *Twister* and recoil in horror, and those who picture themselves right in the thick of the cyclonic action. If you fall into the second category, you might want to think about storm chasing as a career. Yes … a career.

For those not in the know, storm chasers are a rare breed of (questionably mad) folk who dedicate their lives to chasing storms, cyclones and hurricanes with the purpose of witnessing (and often filming) the destruction the violent weather event creates. If you've ever watched a severe weather event unfold on the nightly news, Twitter or a Discovery Channel documentary series, then chances are a storm chaser hopped in a car and risked their life to capture it.

People enter the hectic world of storm chasing for a number of different reasons – curiosity, thrill seeking, science – yet many become storm chasers because they've managed to monetise the process and make a living from pursuing and filming storms and tornadoes. Yes, there is an actual market for storm footage and images. Storm chasers can sell their footage directly to news networks and television production companies, or simply cut the middleman out and create a subscription service that allows footage to be shared directly with the masses. Some talented photographers are able to sell their storm prints (lightning images are a big winner here), while others have been able to create a business running storm-chasing tours, taking general punters out on the chase (I would hate to think what insurance coverage would be needed to run those tours).

Of course, this work is extremely difficult and not for everyone. Firstly, storm chasing is the ultimate definition of seasonal work. Depending on where you are – storm chasers can be found everywhere from Australia to America and Europe – severe weather events don't occur often enough to warrant chasing storms full time. But as a nice little side hustle or part-time enterprise? Sure. Still interested? Then the Great Plains of America is home to a vast area known as 'Tornado Alley' and this is where most storm chasing occurs, so being located there would be wise.

So what does it take to be a storm chaser? An understanding of meteorological terms and weather patterns is a good start, as is having the ability to drive a car and operate technology like cameras, GPS, and technological devices that help interpret weather data. Patience is a huge factor as storm chasing involves lots of sitting around waiting for something to happen. The ability to remain calm under pressure is also essential, so is being able market yourself and your services. There's no point sitting on footage of the storm of the century if you don't know how to sell it or make contacts in the media industry. With no job security or benefits, this career choice is strictly for entrepreneurial, storm-obsessed folk.

When you consider the risks involved, this career is an absolute 'hell no' for most. So unless your loved ones share the same passion for getting close to the kinds of weather events responsible for the deaths of countless people each year, then you'll be putting them through all sorts of torturous worry every hurricane season. It's at times like these that you will need to remind them that construction work actually has one of the highest fatality rates in the world.

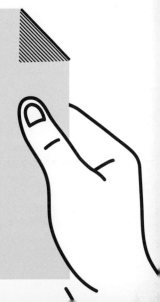

The lowdown

Education or qualifications: None.

Experience required: None.

Training: None.

Restrictions: None.

Street artist

If Banksy is your hero and you've got more than a smidgen of artistic talent, then becoming a street artist is a creative career move that will reward you with everything from accolades to outright scorn. Oh yes, as a street artist you'll never have a dull moment, as this often misunderstood art form tends to be a magnet for controversy. Luckily it also attracts a range of other things, including connection, a sense of community and, for some artists, a really good income.

Street art is a form of visual art that appears in an outdoor setting. Using a wide variety of materials and mediums, street art was once considered an illegal activity only performed by teen vandals with too much time on their hands. Thanks to a growing appreciation of street art, the once-illegal activity now has plenty of scope and has been turned into a legitimate business by savvy artists.

For the purposes of this book, I'm referring to the street (or graffiti) artists who have turned their street art skills into a career and made a business out of creating art in approved outdoor locations, not the people who remain underground, obsessed with not 'selling out', who think that earning a living from graffiti is a no-go because it's an anti-Establishment art form that shouldn't be corrupted by money. Love it or loathe it, it exists and is a valid career these days.

Stencils, paste-ups (posters), painted murals and installations are the most common forms of legal, commissioned street art, and can be found in bars, restaurants, car parks and public parks all over the world, from Los Angeles to Berlin. Realising the huge visual impact street art can have on the public, many governments have engaged with street artists to beautify the city and even convey important messages. As such, street art has flourished in almost every city in the world. From the messages of peace emblazoned on the streets of Belfast to portraits of Nelson Mandela in Soweto, street art has changed the face of many a city.

So how do you monetise your talent for turning brick walls into works of art seen by thousands, if not millions? Like all other careers in the arts, it can be difficult to earn a living from your creativity, especially when you're starting out. Materials like spray paint can be expensive and with murals taking a long time to plan, sketch and pull off, it can be difficult to set your pricing and even more difficult to connect with potential customers when you're an unknown.

The good news is that many talented street artists have managed to turn their passion into a business by marketing themselves to individuals, councils, corporations and brands. From homeowners who want to commission an artist to paint a wall in their backyard to businesses who want a mural as a part of their office, and local councils who want to include street art within their precinct, street artists can make money from a variety of avenues. Some clever street artists have also started teaching workshops and leading street art tours of their neighbourhoods, so being savvy about building new income streams is really an essential part of the business.

Apart from having artistic skills, street artists need to have good listening skills to be able to paint to a brief, marketing knowledge to be able to connect with potential customers, and a good work ethic to be able to stick with a big piece or difficult medium (quitting halfway through a mural is a really bad look). With the best of the best earning six-figure salaries and travelling far and wide to paint in locations around the world, this is an arts career with serious pulling power.

The lowdown

Education or qualifications: None.

Experience required: Experience working with a variety of mediums and materials is essential. Painting an outdoor mural isn't the same as working on a canvas with watercolours.

Training: Some graffiti artists have training in fine arts and other artistic disciplines, but this isn't necessary.

Restrictions: None.

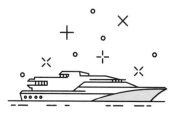

Superyacht captain

While being the captain of any boat would be a genius career move for anyone who loves the ocean, it turns out not all vessels are created equal. Sure, you can think of nothing better than being in command of a whole boat? Sure, but what type? You could join the navy and work your way up to Commander of a war frigate. Or you could buy a commercial vessel and take tourists out to see dolphins. Or you could become the captain of a big cruise liner and ferry thousands of holidaymakers around the Caribbean each summer. Or you could hit a nautical home run and become the captain of a multi-million dollar, privately owned, luxury superyacht.

So what makes a superyacht so super? Generally, superyachts are considered to be any luxury yacht over 80 feet long that is privately owned and staffed all year long with a professional crew. Owned or chartered by very high net worth individuals – think heiresses, royals, celebrities, oil barons, real estate tycoons, mining magnates and the fat cats of the corporate sector – superyachts are found all over the world, but are more common in tax-free havens like Monaco, Bermuda and the Cayman Islands.

Complete with outrageous toys, such as helicopters, mini submarines, jet skis and other pleasure craft, superyachts also regularly feature life 'essentials' like rooftop spas, flat screen televisions with cable, mini theatrettes, and bars stocked with the finest spirits, wines and beers in the world. The owners and their guests expect the best of everything and this extends to the superyacht staff, with everyone from the butler to the chef and, of course, the captain, having to perform to very high standards.

Luckily, superyacht staff are usually renumerated better than the average cruise ship crew and have less cramped living quarters. They also get to experience more remote, exclusive places, as superyacht guests tend to prefer itineraries that avoid the crowds of cruise ship passengers that are disgorged at ports around the world daily.

As on all other boats, the captain is the first link in the chain of command. As such, daily duties involve – but are not limited to – plotting a safe course, steering the ship, contacting marinas about berths, arranging fuel and other supplies, and monitoring the weather. While these are all normal duties for a captain, a superyacht captain gets paid handsomely to play with the latest and greatest toys and navigation equipment, eat food prepared by a classically trained chef, and relax in stylish surroundings shared with only a handful of guests (most of whom are probably celebrities).

So if you love boats and the allure of the open ocean, you could commandeer a fishing trawler but, before you go all *Deadliest Catch* on us, consider the extraordinarily fortunate life and times of a superyacht captain.

The lowdown

Education or qualifications: No degree necessary but you must have years of experience and the appropriate licensing and certifications.

Experience required: Captaining a superyacht isn't an entry-level role. Extensive experience captaining other vessels is required. An understanding of the luxury market and the ability to cater to the (many) needs of the wealthy is also required. Experience working on other superyachts as First Officer is needed before stepping up to the captain's role.

Training: Apart from the qualifications mentioned above, on-the-job training on other superyachts is required to gain an understanding of the specific needs of superyacht owners.

Restrictions: General health and fitness tests apply.

Tattoo artist

Do you have rad drawing skills? Want to work on a canvas unlike any other? Are you down with dealing with the general public all day, every day? Then start sketching – you'll need plenty of practice to become a tattoo artist.

One of the oldest art forms in the world, people have been getting tattoos for centuries. Previously the domain of sailors and hardened criminals, tattoos have hit the mainstream of late with everyone from grannies to straight-laced corporate types getting inked. This is a good thing for tattoo artists, as a growing client base provides more opportunities to make a living. Instead of tattooing crooks and jailbirds, tattoo artists now have a huge pool of customers to service, from newlyweds wanting to ink their names on each other's butts to parents wanting to commemorate their child.

Apart from having great artistic ability, tattoo artists must have many other skills in order to build a career. Having a good understanding of hygienic practices and the ethics of working with people's bodies is essential. Possessing a compassionate, communicative nature is important, especially when dealing with nervous clients (getting inked hurts, okay?) and being able to listen is especially important as if you don't know what your clients want, then you're doomed from the start (and so are they).

The art of tattooing can be learned by attending courses in private colleges, however many artists learn from the greats in an apprenticeship-type situation. With the creative ability to develop their own artistic style, many tattoo artists run their own businesses. From busy tattoo parlours in suburban strip malls to boutique businesses that book out years in advance, tattoo artists can work in a variety of places. Highly sought-after tattoo artists generally have very long waiting lists, command high prices and often travel the world to see clients everywhere from Toyko to Tulsa.

As an art form, tattooing is a high-stakes game, only suited to people who are calm, even-tempered and confident in their abilities. Unlike working on canvas, once a tattoo has been inked on the skin, it's very difficult – not to mention costly and painful – to remove or change, so a certain amount of risk and a huge amount of responsibility comes with this career choice. Anyone who has ever watched episodes of *Tattoo Nightmares* can attest to the horrific damage done by rogues operating under the title of 'tattoo artist'.

If you feel you've got the steady hand, artistic genius and right temperament to be a tattoo artist, then start studying the masters of ink and sketch until your fingers bleed, because you'll need to dedicate years to this craft in order to really nail it. Prison tattoos aside, this isn't a profession for amateurs.

The lowdown

Education or qualifications: No degree necessary.

Experience required: Experience in drawing and inking human bodies is essential. This is not a career for an amateur as the consequences of bad tattoos are huge.

Training: Tattoo schools exist, but many aspiring tattoo artists still apprentice with established tattoo artists in order to learn the trade from the ground up.

Restrictions: None. Although most countries require certification to be able to work in this field.

Taxidermist

Do you have a bit of a morbid streak? Are you fascinated by the animal kingdom? Are you okay with handling dead animals? If you answered yes to those three questions then you might want to consider forging a career in taxidermy.

The art of preserving and restoring deceased animals for display has existed for centuries, with examples of early taxidermy being found in archaeological digs in Egypt. Many people associate creativity with painting watercolours or writing the next bestseller, yet creativity can take many forms. Sure, it may not be the core skill needed to make it in taxidermy (a strong stomach is up there) yet creativity is an integral part of being a successful taxidermist.

After studying the art at a private institution or college, or apprenticing under someone who has worked in taxidermy for years, taxidermists can expect to take their career wherever they like. Such is the intricate, detailed nature of the work, modern taxidermists tend to specialise in one species or type of animal. Working on scaly reptiles is distinctly different from working with feathered birds or furry mammals, so it makes sense for taxidermists to choose one type of animal and stick with it.

Many taxidermists set up their own businesses, offering their services to private clients, such as deer hunters who want a deer head stuffed and mounted for their home, or grieving pet owners who want a constant reminder of Fido in the house. Yes, people do this. In fact, Liberace had all his pets stuffed and arranged around the house after their deaths. Others choose to step into the world of fine art, using their taxidermy skills to create pieces to be shown in public places or sold in private galleries. Other taxidermists work exclusively with museums to preserve animals for display and educational purposes.

Although you'd want to be comfortable with getting up close and personal with dead animals, there are many other skills needed to make it in the world of taxidermy. Apart from knowing all the ins and outs of preserving animals – including the equipment, chemicals, materials and techniques needed – successful taxidermists also need to be able to market themselves to potential clients, have the patience to work on projects that take weeks (or sometimes months) and have a good sense of humour, to put up with all the questions that come when you tell people your career (good luck with dating).

As a career less ordinary, you'll also have to develop a thick skin to deal with concerns from animal rights activists – the sight of a preserved animal is confronting for many people – but on the flipside you'll also get to work with your hands every day, something that most artisans say is highly therapeutic. If you're working independently then you can pick and choose your own projects, working with whomever you wish. You'll be able to keep an ancient art form alive and, if working with museums, preserve species for future generations to learn from and admire. As long as you don't mind other people thinking you're a bit of a weirdo, taxidermy could just be the ticket to a life of freedom, flexibility and creative enrichment.

The lowdown

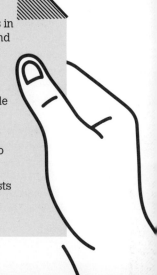

Education or qualifications: Diploma programs in taxidermy are offered by community colleges and other educational institutions around the world.

Experience required: This is the type of career that requires years of experience, either under apprenticeship with a senior taxidermist or while studying the art at college.

Training: Working with skilled taxidermists in an apprenticeship arrangement is a good way to receive on-the-job training.

Restrictions: Some countries require taxidermists to be licensed and have permits to work with certain species.

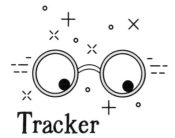

Tracker

While some confused people might ask you to track their lost parcels for them (dispatched from Amazon weeks ago but still not delivered) a professional tracker works on much more important cases than lost book deliveries. Professional trackers have worked on some of the world's biggest search and rescue efforts and crimes that have captured headlines. They don't receive much attention from the press, but their skills are of tremendous value to the community.

Working with the military, law enforcement departments, government agencies and private citizens, professional trackers use a variety of techniques and knowledge to assess the situation and hopefully shed light on what has taken place. Often working with search and rescue teams to locate lost hikers in the wilderness, and helping to find evidence at crime scenes, professional trackers have a very specific set of skills cultivated over years of training.

Obviously having a keen sense of sight, smell and hearing is important, as is having a curious and perceptive nature. Having a good understanding of everything from weather patterns to criminal psychology, trackers are individuals who are dedicated to unravelling mysteries, solving crimes and locating the lost. Noticing a fine strand of hair hanging in a tree branch, finding discarded food wrappers by the side of the road, seeing distinct footprints in mud and observing disturbed shrubs in the wilderness are the types of skills trackers need.

This sort of work isn't for the nine-to-five types, so if you like to be home on the couch watching television at a certain hour or don't like travelling much, then forget professional tracking. As a highly specialised skill, professional trackers often have to mobilise quickly to work on projects in different locations. From mountains to forests, highway verges and river systems, the location is determined by factors out of a tracker's control. Similarly, if a crime is committed at 2am and law enforcement calls through with a request for tracking help, then you can't exactly leave it until the next day to respond after you've had a good sleep in.

Apart from having the ability to track people's movement, trackers need interpersonal skills to be successful. Understanding protocol is paramount, as no one wants someone blundering onto a crime scene, destroying evidence and compromising criminal cases. Being able to work in tandem with others is important, as trackers rarely work alone. Being sensitive to the needs of others is vital, because trackers often work on complicated cases where emotions run high. Having the ability to deal with challenging, traumatic events – like recovering a dead body or failing to find a lost child in the wilderness – is needed, as the work tends to involve unpleasant circumstances.

So how do you become a tracker? There are many pathways to working in tracking. Some trackers come from a military or police background, others are self-taught or taught by family members, and others attend courses to become certified trackers. Either way, the life of a tracker is rich in meaning and life experience. Working outdoors in all kinds of weather and challenging situations is surely tough but being able to contribute to solving crime and returning lost children to worried parents must be immensely satisfying work, well worth dedicating your life to. Plus, you get to avoid working in an office and for some people, that's the greatest triumph of all.

The lowdown

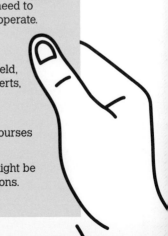

Education or qualifications: Trackers don't need to attend tracking school or college in order to operate.

Experience required: Tracking experience is usually gained by learning from other, more experienced, trackers. Spending time in the field, learning techniques from senior tracking experts, is one of the best ways to gain experience in this role.

Training: While rare, privately run tracking courses can be found in many countries.

Restrictions: Some criminal record checks might be required to work on certain cases and situations.

Travel writer

Envy alert! It's sickening to think about, but currently there are legions of travel writers all over the world getting paid to do all sorts of very cool things. They are sipping cocktails on superyachts in the Caribbean, witnessing sunrises from the top of Mount Kilimanjaro, eating steaming bowls of pho in Vietnam and snorkelling the Great Barrier Reef in Australia. Some are camped out in tents in Canada's national parks while others are holed up in European luxury hotels sampling things like pillow menus, the butler service and in-house cheese caves.

Being paid to travel the globe rates as one of the most sought-after careers, yet it's also one that many people mistakenly believe is out of their reach. Well, know this: travel writers aren't unicorns. I should know – I am one. But there was a time when I believed that travel writing was nothing more than a mirage. And gee, was I wrong. I'm here to tell you that there are thousands of people currently being paid to go on vacation, so why not you?

Whether you choose to forge a freelance career selling your work to the media, nab a coveted in-house role with the travel section of a national newspaper, or build a popular travel blog with thousands of followers, earning a living from travel writing is entirely possible. You can get a degree in journalism, go for an internship with your local newspaper, apply for roles at guidebook publishers, or you can say to hell with all that and just write and pitch your stories to websites, magazines and newspapers. You could even write the next bestseller that takes the literary world by storm and inspires a generation of people to travel.

The range of experiences on offer as a travel writer is so varied you'll never be bored. I've been paid to sail to Antarctica on a yacht, walk through the Australian desert, climb mountains in Morocco, sip tea in Sri Lanka, handfeed giraffes in Africa and sleep in a palace in India. But above all, the greatest gift I've been given as a travel writer is the freedom to explore the world and then share it with others through my words and images, followed closely by avoiding the nine-to-five grind.

Sure, there are downsides to the job. There's jet lag, homesickness, airport delays and jealous friends, but that's a small price to pay for getting paid to travel (plus all the frequent flyer miles are pretty sweet, too).

The lowdown

Education or qualifications: No formal education requirements needed but a degree in journalism or other writing qualifications would help.

Experience required: No official experience necessary but, similar to many other publishing and media roles, building up a strong list of published work (or clips) will help with pitching and job seeking. Oh, and without travel experience you aren't going to be much of a travel writer, so get out there and experience the world.

Training: No training necessary. Travel writers with no prior experience get their work published all the time, as do seasoned professionals with 40+ years in the business.

Restrictions: If you can travel and write, then you can be a published travel writer.

Truffle hunter

Here is a rare job that manages to combine three of the things that make most humans very happy: dogs, food and nature. For anyone who despises the thought of being cooped up all day in an office under fluorescent lighting, the role of a truffle hunter may have major appeal.

A job that dates back 4000 years and formerly the domain of the pig, truffle hunting is now mainly completed by dogs (mostly because dogs can be trained to find but not eat a truffle, while pigs are more likely to gobble it up on the spot). The talented canines find truffles both in the wild and on truffle farms that have miles and miles of truffles hidden under the earth. With this prized fungus fetching big prices in the food industry, truffle hunting can be quite lucrative for the human in charge of the dog.

There are hundreds of different truffle varieties found around the world, so this type of work can be done wherever truffles grow – from Croatia to Italy, France, Australia, New Zealand, the UK and the Unites States of America. All that truffle hunters require is a reasonable amount of fitness, a dog that has been trained to seek out the truffle scent, and a good understanding of what makes a good truffle (a rotten truffle is worthless and an unripened one won't command a good price).

A typical day for a truffle hunter involves going out into the wild or working on a farm where the trees have been inoculated with truffle spores in the off-season. Walking around in a methodical pattern with their dogs, truffle hunters encourage their canines to sniff out the treasures that lie hidden below. The dogs are rewarded with treats or a game of fetch for every truffle they unearth. At the end of the day, the truffle hunter takes their haul to be weighed and is paid the market rate, which fluctuates depending on demand.

Luckily, truffles have started to become incredibly popular on menus around the world, and prices have increased. Cha-ching!

As seasonal work – the truffle season is limited to a few months of the year – many truffle hunters train their dogs to put their noses to work in other ways. From working at airports to detect contraband items within luggage, or with wildlife conservationists to locate rare species in the wild, truffle hunters can moonlight in the off-season if they wish. Alternatively, some can make enough money in one truffle season to sustain them for the entire year. Now that's one hell of a truffle shuffle!

The lowdown

Education or qualifications: No formal education requirements are required to hunt truffles.

Experience required: This is a learn-as-you-go type of job, so learning from an experienced truffle hunter would be a wise move to get your foot in the door.

Training: On-the-job training is the most common way to get experience in truffle hunting. Dog handling and training courses would help with the dog management side of things, although this does come naturally to some.

Restrictions: None. Although being reasonably fit would help.

Volcanologist

Krakatoa. Vesuvius. St Helens. Etna. Kīlauea. It would be hard to find a geological phenomenon as feared and revered as the volcano. Volcanoes are a force of nature responsible for some of the most catastrophic events in the history of the world. We are fascinated by them, despite the destruction they have wreaked, and often turn them into tourist attractions and even a source of green energy, when they are not spewing hot ash and rivers of lava into the atmosphere. Many of us might have a gentle curiosity for the volcano – no doubt sparked by making a volcano diorama in school – some have an obsession. And it is those people who tend to end up studying for many years to become experts in volcanoes, or volcanologists. Most volcanologists work on monitoring volcanic activity and completing risk assessments for government departments, others choose to take teaching roles at universities, and some do both throughout their career.

The road to volcanic glory may sound explosive, but this is a career that requires a hefty amount of study. If you have no interest in academia, then forget following a career in volcanology. The same goes if you suck at mathematics or don't have the discipline required to study hard. After completing a degree in geology, most volcanologists go on to study a PhD, so you're looking at a good six to eight years of study before having the base requirements for the job. After you've finished your courses, jobs in volcanology are few and far between, although it does help to live in a country or state with many active volcanoes – for instance, Indonesia, Hawaii, the Philippines, Japan or Italy.

Getting up close and personal with volcanoes is an integral (and risky) part of the job. Field work involves everything from collecting lava and gas samples to assessing ground deformation in areas known for having volcanic activity. As any scientist will tell you, field work is a richly valued part of the job. Despite this, volcanologists don't spend all of their time hanging around smouldering volcanic craters. Many hours are spent in an office or studying, reading, researching and writing. Giving lectures at events and conferences is also part of the job, as is preparing briefings in the lead up to and aftermath of a large volcanic event.

When it comes to safety, this is one of the riskier science careers out there. Most volcanologists end up in very close proximity to eruptions – partly because they love it, partly because it's their job – and deaths in the field have occurred. The 1991 eruption of Mount Unzen in Japan ended the lives of 43 people, including three volcanologists. So it's official: volcanology is as badass as it gets.

The lowdown

Education or qualifications: A degree in geology, followed by postgraduate study in volcanology – a PhD is generally required.

Experience required: Extensive experience completing field work and research in the area, usually gained during undergraduate and postgraduate study in geology.

Training: On-the-job training in research techniques and best-practice field work occurs while completing your tertiary studies.

Restrictions: None.

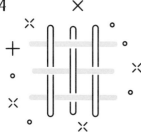

Weaver

Do you think weaving is something that people only did back in medieval times? Wrong! Weaving is a creative pursuit enjoyed by millions of people all over the world. Yep, weaver fever is a thing, and it's made people hit the loom pretty hard of late. Some people weave just for fun, but some creative souls have managed to turn it into a full-blown career. And you could too.

Weavers can use a manual (traditional) loom or a computerised one to create woven fabrics for practical use and decoration. Some weavers work in textile factories using mechanised looms, but many others build their own businesses in the craft weaving sector. These craft weavers tend to use traditional looms and, although harder to use, these looms are perfect for creating bespoke pieces and works of art.

Thanks to trends in design and home décor moving towards woollen textiles, wall hangings and other handmade pieces over mass-produced soft furnishings, the art of weaving is enjoying a bit of a renaissance.

This growing appreciation has led to an explosion in the number of people picking up looms and attending weaving workshops and courses. Most are learning the art as a hobby, but many have been able to create profitable small businesses out of their talent for rearranging wool into beautiful works of art.

Having a creative streak, a good eye for colour and the patience to work towards a project that will take time to complete are all essential skills for anyone who wants to be a craft weaver. Marketing your work is also a huge part of making it as a modern weaver. Many weavers uses platforms like Etsy to sell their work; others sell to stores and boutiques, at markets or via their own website. The work of some weavers even ends up in art galleries.

Depending on your skill level and ability to market yourself to the world, weaving can be quite profitable.

The realities of weaving may make you run in the opposite direction. With earning a good living from weaving being quite a tenuous prospect and many, many hours going into the creation of the works you need to sell, this is the type of career you'd only pursue for the sheer love of it. But thankfully it's not all living hand-to-mouth and hunching over a loom into the wee hours of the morning. Some of the best parts of weaving as a business include having the flexibility to work from home or your own studio, the freedom to create whatever you want, and the joy of having the beautiful fruits of your labour hanging in galleries, homes and other spaces.

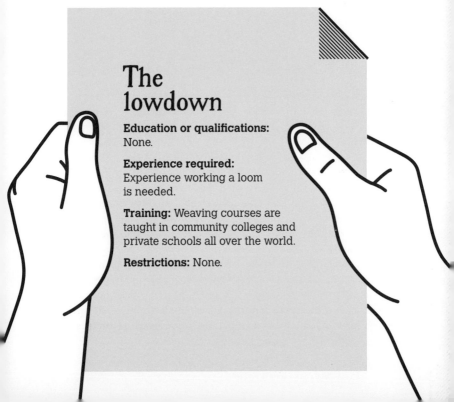

The lowdown

Education or qualifications:
None.

Experience required:
Experience working a loom
is needed.

Training: Weaving courses are
taught in community colleges and
private schools all over the world.

Restrictions: None.

Wig maker

Thought wigs were something you could just buy from a costume shop at Halloween? Sure, there are many cheap, mass-produced, synthetic wigs out there just perfect for your next fancy dress party, but apart from those types of wigs, there's a whole other scene of custom wig making and it's a pretty damn fascinating world.

Mass-produced wigs might be perfect when you want to dress up as Cher, but the itchy, obviously fake, manufactured fibres of synthetic wigs just don't cut it when you're talking about wigs needed for theatre and film productions. Mostly made with human hair or animal fibres, and threaded by hand, strand-by-strand, the profession of wig making is a highly intricate one; a true art form that is chronically overlooked by the masses.

From making outrageous wigs for Broadway shows, to curly moustaches for period films, and even underarm hair for a comedy series, in the entertainment industry highly skilled wig makers get to work on a variety of productions, creating a wide range of wigs. Not convinced that wig making is that important? Consider Gandalf from *Lord of the Rings* without his epic white beard, or Daenerys from *Game of Thrones* without her braided, snow-white tresses. Each series of *Game of Thrones* alone used an estimated 20–30 wigs, so yes, wigs are kind of a big deal in the movie and television business.

Apart from film, theatre and television work, many wig makers also work with private clients who have experienced hair loss due to medical conditions, chemotherapy treatment or age. This type of work, while less high profile, is extremely rewarding, as contributing to the quality of life of a cancer patient or person with alopecia provides a great deal of job satisfaction. A highly personal and sometimes emotional process, wig making for private clients is normally very hands-on, and therefore requires good interpersonal skills. Empathy not your strong suit? Best keep film and television wig making in your sights then.

So what does it take to be a successful wig maker? Well, threading thousands of strands of human hair, one by one, requires a great deal of patience and the ability to focus on a repetitive task for many hours. Knowing how to stick to a brief is essential, as there's no point freestyling it and making a blonde bob for a client who wanted flowing, chestnut tresses. Wig making for film and television requires an understanding of the film process, so you'd want to love movies to get into this game.

If you think you've got what it takes to be a wig maker, then apprenticing with a master wig maker is a good way to learn about the process, increase your skills and get a foot in the door of the industry. You might receive low pay in the beginning but, once you've earned your stripes and built up a solid wig portfolio, you can take your work wherever you like. Whether that's fitting a toupee on a celebrity's head, tailoring a new look for a cancer patient, or handcrafting a chunky moustache for a seventies movie remake – it's up to you.

The lowdown

Education or qualifications: No tertiary education or formal qualifications are required, although wig-making courses, sometimes as a part of hair and make-up courses, are offered in many major cities.

Experience required: Beginners commonly gain experience through an apprenticeship. Professional wig makers have years of experience in the industry before landing film and television work.

Training: Some wig makers attend wig-making courses, others choose to receive on-the-job training by completing apprenticeships with master wig makers.

Restrictions: None.

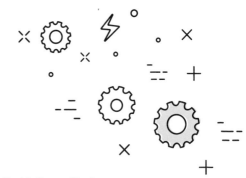

Smith Street Books

Published in 2018 by Smith Street Books
Melbourne | Australia
smithstreetbooks.com

ISBN: 978-1-925418-42-2

CIP data is available from the National Library of Australia.

Publisher: Paul McNally
Project manager: Aisling Coughlan
Editor: Vanessa Pellatt
Design and illustrations: Stephanie Spartels

Printed & bound in China by C&C Offset Printing Co., Ltd.

Book 51
10 9 8 7 6 5 4 3 2 1

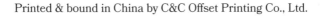